Praise for Just Around The Corner

"Barbara Grahn gives a wonderful gift to Baby Boomers. Her interactive guide will be a great companion if career questions keep you up at night."

> *Beverly Kaye, CEO/Founder Career System International, Co-Author of "Love It Don't Leave It: 26 ways to Get What You Want at Work"*

"Baby Boomers take heart, finally a career guide just for you."

> *Bob Rosner, author of "Gray Matters" and internationally syndicated Working Wounded columnist*

"What a fabulous tool to work through one's roadblocks when embarking on a new career. Immensely helpful!"

> *Alice Illingworth, 20 year veteran educator in pursuit of a new creative career*

"Just Around the Corner is great for Baby Boomers because it's targeted at their specific issues and questions. The process of finding a new career isn't the same for everyone ... this book helps a specific population of folks with exploring their next path. Highly recommend it!"

> *Kathleen Sexton, COMPASS Career Program Manager, Stanford University*

"Working through this book was a great way to identify what was missing in my career. It had invaluable tips on how to explore potential new careers."

> *Mike Sneddon, CEO and soon-to-be golf shop owner*

"Retiring from my career was risky, but pursuing a new career that has always intrigued me will keep me engaged for the rest of my life. This book helps!"

> *Joe Flemming, Retired software engineer, now studying Eastern Medicine in Hawaii*

Just Around The Corner

A Baby Boomer's Guide to a Career or Job Change

By

Barbara Grahn

authorHOUSE

1663 Liberty Drive, Suite 200
Bloomington, Indiana 47403
(800) 839-8640
www.authorhouse.com

First published by AuthorHouse 09/01/04

ISBN: 1-4184-7090-2 (sc)

Library of Congress Control Number: 2004095489

Printed in the United States of America
Bloomington, Indiana

This book is printed on acid-free paper.

Pencil Illustration by Barbara Grahn.

Table of Contents

Acknowledgments

A special thanks to Valerie Beeman, Betsy Matthews, Susy Ruitenbeck, Kim Schilling, and Yvonne Wolters who edited and shaped my book – I could not have done it without you! For the unfaltering support of my husband, Dennis, and son, Matt – you made it easy for me to write. And to Susan Maltz who opened the door to this new career path.

Barbara

I believe the second half of one's life is meant to be better than the first. The first half is finding out how you do it. And the second half is enjoying it.

Frances Lear

Introduction

"Jobs and careers should not be life sentences. Periodically assess your career health and feel free to make changes when necessary."

Ron Krannich, author of "Change your Job, Change your Life"
Impact Publications 2000

If you are a Baby Boomer, born between 1946 and 1964, then I wrote this book with you in mind. As a Baby Boomer you may have had multiple jobs, one or two careers, started your own company, or worked 30 years in a single job. During your working years you may have taken time off work to raise a family, experienced a layoff, or taken a sabbatical. All of these circumstances have shaped how you feel about work – what you like to do, where you like to work, and whom you like to work with. It could be that you are no longer passionate about your current job, like I was, and needed a change. Or you have been out of the workplace and have no idea how to get back in. Or you just want to try something new.

Reading this book can help you plan a job change (a change of job within the same career), or plan a total career change (change a profession or field). I won't tell you what career you should choose, but how to discover that yourself. Only you can decide what career fits you the best. Others can help you along the way, but ultimately the choice is yours. In this book, I give you tools to help you know yourself better, explore career options, make decisions and set goals, and then I give you information on how to get the job that you really want.

It's important to explore all possible career options, to keep an open mind, to know what you want, and learn how to get there. The career self-management skills I teach in this book can be used throughout your life. In fact, it's a good idea to revisit this book from time to time to see if you are still on the right track. Reading and using this book is just the first step to finding a fulfilling career that you love. I did!

Foreword

How can the next forty years of your life be interesting, productive, and rewarding? Embarking on a career change can take you on an amazing journey of self-discovery and finding your true direction.

Barbara Sher, author of, *It's Only Too Late If You Don't Start Now* (Delecorte Press 1994*)* has this to say*:*

You're turning a big corner all right, and walking down a new street. As a matter of fact, this is one of life's most significant turns. But the minute you step around that corner what you're going to see will astonish you.

You're not heading for any kind of decline. In fact, you're about to embark on an amazing new beginning. The era you're entering is so different from your first forty years it's completely justifiable to call it your second life.

You start paying attention to your dreams to decide how you want to live. You begin to write the books that are in you, or go into the theater and become an actor like you've always wanted, or you become an Arctic explorer, or a business owner, or you build the community you've always known was possible, or you head out and see the world you've always longed to see.

In other words, you start to live your life to suit who you really are. You go after your own dreams with new respect and a clear mind because you don't have to prove anything. You're not trying to impress anyone. The top item on your list of priorities says, "Find the life I was born to live." Everything else comes after that.

Chapter 1

It's just around the Corner

Have you worked for 10 or 20 years in the same job and now feel bored and unchallenged?

Have you been out of the workplace for many years and don't know how to get back on the career track?

Have you been "downsized" or "repositioned" and want to consider your next career steps?

Have you lost passion for your current career?

Will you soon retire and don't know what to do with your time?

Well, help is just around the corner! Waking up each morning excited about how you spend your day is everyone's dream. Whether you want to start a new career or find some passion for what you do, getting to know yourself, exploring your options, and planning a course of action are the keys to finding a career that fits you the best.

Have a pencil ready—you'll use it throughout the book!

A Baby Boomer's Dilemma

Alicia spent the last 20 years teaching high school. Although she loves children and is a master teacher, she no longer feels a sense of satisfaction going to work each day. In fact, she feels unchallenged and bored. She chose a teaching career because people said she was great with kids. Her real passion was fashion design and she used to create unique and trendy clothing from scratch. All this went by the wayside as she pursued her teaching career. Now what can she do?

Todd went into the family business as an attorney. He has worked the last 30 years in the law firm and now leads the company. He's great at his job, but has never felt an ounce of passion for the work. When he was young he always dreamed about working in the sports industry, he even wanted to play professional baseball. He feels trapped in his job due to family and financial reasons. Is there any hope for him?

As a Baby Boomer, you may have been in the workforce many years – some of you have worked over 35 years – and now you may want or need a change. Although many of you have remained in the same job throughout your lives, others may have changed jobs within the same profession, or even changed careers multiple times. Still others have taken time off to raise children and now want to enter the workforce. But where do you start?

Typically when thinking about a career change, you have to ask yourself these questions:

Do I have the freedom to move to another geographical location to get a job?

If your answer is yes, your choices for a new career and choice jobs are wide open. You could explore the best places to work, the top employers, most livable cities and towns. Also check unemployment rates and growth opportunities in the fields that interest you. If your answer is no, this might be the next question you ask yourself:

Should I continue my present career?

Think about what it would take for you to stay in your present job. Would a job redesign make the job more interesting? Is moving to a different job within the company an option? What would entice you to stay in the job – flexible hours, part time work or a higher salary? Maybe a sabbatical? One of these options may be the perfect choice for you if you are not ready to make a career change. For example, Alicia's profession is teaching and she has worked all her life as a high school teacher. Instead of changing her career, she may decide to work in a corporate training department, as an educational consultant, or for the U.S. Department of Education. Using this book to assess her skills, values, and interests, learning to explore her career options, and rewriting her resume would help her prepare for a job change.

Do I want to re-enter the workforce in the same career that I had many years ago?

If this is what you want to do, it will be crucial that you re-explore the career. How has the job changed? What skills are now needed to get the job done? Is specific training or a degree now needed to obtain the job? It will also be important to use this book to explore how *you* have changed. What are your strengths? Have your workplace values changed and do they still match the workplace of today? What new experiences and skills can you offer an employer?

Should I start a new career?

Answering yes to this question gives you many options depending on your personal circumstances. If you want to start a new career, you will have to decide if you want to work for others or work for yourself by starting a business. This is only one of the decisions you will have to make as you explore career options. If you have been laid off or recently retired, why not try something new? When the economy is recessed and unemployment is high, broadening your job search to include an alternative career can be a wise move. Regardless of whether you are retiring or not, it is essential to try and incorporate the things you love into a new job or career.

How do you go about making a career change? If you don't have financial restrictions, you may want to consider volunteer work to experience a different career. Or you may be able to go back to school for retraining or begin an internship to learn a new job. If finances are a consideration, you might try working one job part-time, especially if you need to continue working in your current job while pursuing other career options. This book will help you know yourself better – your skills, interests, values, working style, accomplishments, and passion, and then guide you as you explore careers through informational interviews and networking.

What is a Baby Boomer?

As a Baby Boomer, you and I have unique career perspectives and needs. This book can help you understand yourself and help you meet any career challenges you may have identified. What is a Baby Boomer? We Baby Boomer were born between 1946 and 1964. The first Baby Boomers turned 50 on January 1, 1996 and unlike older generations, many have delayed marrying and having children. This often means that we have to work longer and later in life to support our children. Some of us may not be able to prepare for retirement until our children are nearly grown. We are more likely to have more than one career, and work for more employers than our parents did. Working for multiple employers can be problematic because pensions may end up smaller. Unfortunately, to compensate for this smaller pension, we may have to work many more years before we can afford to retire. In fact, according to a recent American Association of Retired Persons (AARP) study, almost 70% of people over 45 now say they plan to continue working after they are 65. A Roper Starch Worldwide survey estimates an even higher number – 80%. So, if you, as a Baby Boomer, are looking for a career change, now may be the time to make that change. You may have many more years to work and opportunities abound in the workplace today. If you don't know where to start, working through the assessments in this book to develop a career profile will help you identify patterns that can lead you to career options that you had not previously considered. This will start you down the road to obtaining that career you always wanted.

A New World of Work

As Baby Boomers, we have seen the world of work change dramatically in the last 30 years. There are many jobs that no longer exist and an abundance of newly created jobs for our technologically oriented world. Jobs have evolved and the technical skill it takes to do many jobs has changed. Just the introduction of the computer changed most workplace processes and practices in a dramatic way.

Here are some interesting new jobs today:

Nanotechnologist – makes machines at a molecular scale; creates virus-size robots using carbon fibers stronger than steel

Plant Geneticist – using biotech tools, introduces proteins into plants that can be used to fight human viruses

Virtual Reality Architect – using computers, creates designs that have not yet been built

Business Process Analyst – determines and implements the best process to enhance the function of databases, computer systems, or other business applications

Aquaculturist – farmer who breeds or grows shellfish, crustaceans, or fin fish for profit

Organizational Development Specialist – helps companies or departments perform at their best by enhancing or changing employee practices, work processes, the environment, culture, or structure

Bioinformatics Analyst – a profession pairing biology and computer science; data produced by the Human Genome Project (gene sorting) are analyzed and studied for possible clues and eventual cures for diseases

Geospatial Technologist – uses surveying tools from space to manage forests, map natural hazards, design roads, study global charge, or design cellular phone networks

These are just a few of the new and exciting jobs in this millennium. The number of new job titles increases daily! In fact, 70 percent of today's jobs will disappear by the year 2050. Keep an open mind as you explore your options because the jobs of today may not exist tomorrow.

Job Trends

So what jobs are out there? What fields should you consider if you want to change your career? Some of the fastest growing occupations reported by the U.S. Bureau of Labor Statistics for the years 2000-2010 are:

Computer Software Engineers, applications and systems
Computer Support Specialists
Network and Computer Systems Administrators
Network Systems and Data Communication Analysts
Desktop Publishers
Database Administrators
Personal and Home Care Aides
Computer Systems Analysts
Medical Assistants

As the oldest Baby Boomers retire, Governing magazine reports ten occupations where replacement of workers will be greatest between 2003 and 2008:

Elementary School Teachers

Registered Nurses
Administrators in education and related fields
Administrators in public administration
Financial Managers
Lawyers
Social Workers
Teacher's Aides
Plumbers, Pipe fitters and Steamfitters
Postal Clerks (except Mail Carriers)

Job openings and salaries in healthcare, high tech (especially computer and data processing), and the management and public relations fields are expected to increase. In fact, half of all federal workers will be eligible to retire by 2006. So if you want to change your career to these specific fields, the time to do that is right now. This isn't to say that these are the only fields that will be hiring in the future, just that these jobs are the fastest growing in the U.S. today. Don't discount the career you really dream about just because it isn't on the list of fastest growing occupations. In fact it may be that you want a job less demanding than your current job, or even a lower level job that may increase your overall happiness by giving you time to pursue other interests. As you read this book, keep an open mind and develop a broad list of career options.

You may ask, won't the younger generation get most of the new jobs that come up? Not necessarily! The workforce is changing. The number of 16 - 24 year olds entering the job market has been declining since 1975, so employers are drawing from a smaller pool of younger applicants for these jobs. This means that there is ample opportunity to change a job or change a career. In addition, Baby Boomers have more experience and skills than younger workers just entering the workforce.

Higher Level of Skills Needed

If you decide to explore new jobs in the high tech and healthcare areas, be aware that a higher level of skills, both technical skills and more transferable skills, will be needed. This could mean that additional technical training may be necessary to obtain these jobs. But you probably have many of the valuable **transferable** skills you will need for the job:

- Communication (good verbal and writing skills; computer literate; and fluency in a second language)
- Problem-solving (take initiative and seek solutions)
- Participating in teams (work well and cooperatively with others)
- Continuous learning (keeping skills current and learning additional skills)

These are just some of the skills needed for the 21st century. They are skills that are transferable from job to job and most people have some degree of competence in each of these areas. Focus on improving your skills in these four areas. Typically, with each new job, you will build or enhance your skills. Self-assessment (knowing yourself) and continuous skill building are key steps in choosing a career that's right for you.

What skills do you already have? Or do you think that you have no skills at all? Starting out with no core skills to perform a job is rare. Everyone has skills, although some may have more developed skills than others. Skills are acquired abilities to do something through practice or training. You do not have to acquire your skills through paid work; life experiences and volunteer work are important sources of skill acquisition. Think about what you are good at today and write these things on the lines below. Here are some examples:

Organizing people	Fixing things	Planning projects
Designing things	Solving problems	Leading a group
Speaking in public	Organizing events	Writing
Cooking	Driving	Gardening

My Skills:

_____

_____

_____

_____

_____

_____

Many of these skills are needed for the jobs of today and most likely will be needed for the jobs of tomorrow. It is crucial that you become flexible and gain skills that will benefit you for the jobs of tomorrow. Keep these skills in mind when you start Chapter 4 on skill identification.

Developing a Career Profile

You want to make a career or job change, so what do you do? Developing a career profile of who you are and what you want to do with your life is a crucial first step in finding work that you will enjoy for many years to come. If you can think and plan while looking at the big picture, the choice jobs can be yours. So don't just choose a job title and leave it at that. You also have to know if the job suits you and explore the career thoroughly. It's important to learn these skills so that you can manage your career throughout your life.

I've designed this book as an interactive tool to guide you in your search for the perfect career. Each section contains activities to help you find out more about your interests, skills, motivation, values, and working style, and help you explore the options available to you when choosing a career. Then I help you make a decision, and give you information on how to apply for and get the job you most desire.

When you are exploring your career choices, it's important to begin your planning by thinking big and then narrowing down your options. The diagram below will help you identify the areas you need to explore. As you embark on your career search, choose a place to start, but know that at any time in your life you can re-enter the career planning process and continue your journey. The section called "Know Who You Are" is a good place to begin. It is important to learn about yourself and what you have to offer the world before you move on to the next step.

Managing your Career

Learn the skills to:

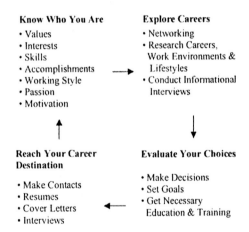

How to Use This Book

This book will cover all of these elements to manage your career. Chapters 1 through 5 focus on knowing who you are:

- Your values
- Your interests
- Your skills

- Your accomplishments
- Your experience
- Your working style
- Your passions and motivation

Chapter 6 helps you choose careers that fit you the best

- How to find patterns in your Career Profile
- Choosing careers to explore

Chapter 7 focuses on exploring the world of work:

- Networking
- Research careers, work environments and lifestyles
- Conduct informational interviews

Chapter 8 helps you evaluate your choices:

- Financial considerations and other options
- Make decisions
- Set goals and make action plans
- Get necessary education and training

Chapter 9 provides you with tools to reach your career destination:

- Your job search
- Create resumes
- Write cover letters
- Prepare for interviews

This book will give you the needed skills to continue job exploration throughout your entire life. It will help you discover, create or refine a career that fits you the best. Following these steps worked for me, they'll certainly work for you too!

Chapter 2

Take It Step By Step

Once you know who you are, you don't have to worry any more.
Nikki Giovanni

The first step in your quest for a new career or for changing your current job is to know yourself better. Some of you may want to make a complete career change. An example of this would be moving from legal work to healthcare, or from education to business management. Others may want to change jobs within the field. For example, changing your engineering job from product design to structural engineering, or from the newspaper editing department to the marketing department.

Getting to know yourself is the best way to choose the right career or job for you. Be ready with a pencil to complete the activities in each chapter. This will help you identify the interests, skills, values, and working styles that will enable you to know yourself better. Once you understand the essence of who you are, it will be easier to choose a career direction that fits.

Get to Know Yourself

Knowing yourself includes identifying your values or personal standards. For example:

- Do you want a job helping others?
- Do you want a job where you make lots of money?
- Do you want a job that helps the community or the environment?

It's important to prioritize your values to help you choose a career that best fits you.

Knowing yourself also includes identifying your interests and preferences:

- Do you like working with data, or would you prefer to work with ideas?
- Do you like working with people, or would you rather work with machines?

It's important to know what you prefer, so that the job you choose reflects your interests.

Knowing yourself includes identifying your skills. For example:

- Can you organize an event flawlessly?
- Are you good at talking to people?
- Are you good at fixing machines?

Knowing your skills will help you decide on a job and improve your chances for success. An inventory of your skills and accomplishments can help you write an effective resume and cover letter and help you clinch the interview. Your working style, motivation, and passion will also play a part in your career choice.

The next few chapters will help you get to know yourself better. After you have identified who you are, it will be time to explore job options that fit with your skills, values, interests, and goals. Be sure to use the Career Profile at the end of the book to keep track of your answers. It will help you identify patterns and make choices when the time comes to choose a career.

STOP! **Locate the Career Profile at the end of the book.**

Let's begin by filling in the Career Profile, starting with your life goals, past accomplishments, and values.

What is your Life Goal?

Through the years you have probably made many life goals – retire before you are 50, become a millionaire by 30, have a large family with five children, become successful in your career, or live in a large house in the country. You may have articulated your life goals, or not. Your life goals may have changed through the years or remained the same. You may have attained your life goal and now need to make a new one. Maybe you have no idea what your life goals are. If you have no idea, it's important to begin to think about life goals, so that you can incorporate them in your career planning. If you haven't thought about your life goals, think about them right now because now is the time to integrate these goals into the career you choose.

People choose what they want to be for many reasons. Be sure you have a reason for choosing your work– don't just take the easiest path. Many people don't find their ideal job because they haven't identified their life goals, let alone their interests, values, and skills. Think big to help you find your direction. Explore all possibilities and stay open-minded.

What can a life goal be?
- Your life goal may involve being healthy, happy, and having enough money to travel the world.
- Your life goal may be to get your children through college and married, and have a large, happy family to nurture you in your retirement.
- Your life goal may be to live your life in a quiet place, in a quiet way, by yourself.

When you choose your life goals, don't give up on your dreams, but be honest and realistic when identifying goals.

Write down your life goal(s):

_____

_____

_____

_____

_____

Your life goal is just one piece of the puzzle. Knowing your life goal can help you make a crucial decision when choosing among the many jobs or careers out there.

STOP! **Transfer this life goal to the Career Profile at the end of the book.**

Accomplishments and Achievements

I'm sure there are many things that you have accomplished in your life. This is the time to write down the things you have done that makes you most proud. These may be activities that gave you a sense of satisfaction or a sense of accomplishment, and were things that you enjoyed doing and were successful.

Your accomplishments can help you identify skills in which you excel. They can help you pinpoint a field of work that you had not previously considered. They can also be used in your resume or cover letter to help you get a future job. Do not limit yourself to job related accomplishments. If you are talented in other areas such as drawing, quilting, volunteer activities, or there are school subjects in which you excelled, be sure to write down accomplishments or achievements in those areas, too. Here are some examples:

• I designed the plans for our kitchen remodel and managed the project, completing the job in the time allotted.

• I entered a juried art show and won an award in the mixed media category.

• I completed my B.S. degree attending school at night, while working part-time and raising my young son.

• I won an award for a web-based training site I developed while in my current position.

Your accomplishment(s):

_____

_____

_____

_____

_____

_____

_____

STOP! **Transfer your most significant accomplishments to the Career Profile at the end of the book. You will be revisiting these accomplishments in future chapters.**

What Do You Value the Most?

Meaning is not something you stumble across, like the answer to a riddle or the prize in a treasure hunt. Meaning is something you build into your own life.

– John W. Gardner, Founder of Common Cause and former Secretary of Health, Education, and Welfare

Now that you have identified your life goals and past accomplishments, think about your values. What are values? Values are the personal standards that are important to each of us. They are the things in life you care about most that form the basis for your lives. You have both personal values and work-related values – things you value personally and things you value in the workplace. Look back at the choices you've made in your life and think about how many times your values have driven your decisions. Did you take a job for a specific reason? Why did you choose a friend? Why did you end a friendship? The answers to these types of questions help you identify your values. Values give your life meaning.

Values are not easily left behind when you leave for work each day. They guide you at home and work, and everywhere in between. For example, perhaps you value helping others or having social status, or helping the environment or making money. In the workplace you may value working outdoors or in an unstructured indoor workplace, working as part of a team or working alone.

Your values can and do change over your lifetime, so it's important to reassess your values from time to time. You should be able to clearly identify your values before you move on to making a career choice or a career change.

Identify Your Values

Let's identify your values now. The goal in this next section is to identify your **four** most important values.

Read each value below and check the appropriate box to rate it from 1 to 4 (1 = not important, 2 = rarely important, 3 = sometimes important, and 4 = very important).

	not important		very important	
My Environment	1	2	3	4
Job security (keep my job for a long time)				
Unstructured environment (do my work in a flexible way)				
Structured environment (do my work in a specific way at a specific time)				
Time to spend with family/friends				
Quiet workplace				
Active, bustling workplace				

	not important		very important	
	1	2	3	4

Public contact (interact with customers)

Location of my choosing (work at home or office)

High salary/benefits

Risk (potential to fail, but high rewards if I succeed)

Flexible hours (choose the hours and days of the week or month I do my job)

Low stress at work

High stress job (lots of reward)

Outdoor workplace (all or part of my day)

Indoor workplace (all or part of my day)

Diverse workplace (work with many types of people)

	not important		very important	
Relationships	1	2	3	4
Leading and influencing others				
Working as part of a team				
Working independently				
Having status with others				
Collaborating with others to make decisions				
Competitive workplace				
Non-competitive workplace				
Fun place to work				
Responsible for work of others				
High level of communication with others				
Feeling needed and appreciated by colleagues				

	not important		very important	
	1	2	3	4

Loyalty (loyal to other workers and the employer)

Honesty (honest workers and employer)

Compassion (your co-workers and employer care about you)

Being popular with others

	not important		very important	
Work Content	1	2	3	4

Challenging work

Help the environment

Invent new things

Creative work

Work tasks change often

	not important		very important	
	1	2	3	4
Same work every day				
Physical challenge				
Help others				
Help the community				
Work with new technology				
Learning opportunities (learn by doing)				
Take initiative (action needed without direction from supervisor)				
Advance my career (job leads to a higher level job)				
Expertise (advanced knowledge needed to do the job)				
Minimal knowledge needed to do the job				
Make independent decisions				
Intellectual stimulation				

Next:

1. Look back at the choices marked highest (checkbox #4). Draw a star ☆ next to the 8 to 10 items you rated most important to you.

2. Circle your top four values from the starred items and write them below:

1.   3.
2.   4.

Now that you have carefully chosen the values that are important to you, is there one value that you will never compromise? One that is so important that it must be in your job? If there is, write it in the box below:

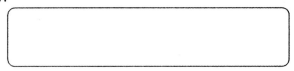

STOP! **Add these four values to your Profile at the end of the book, putting the most important value first**.

Your Personal Values

In addition to identifying the values that you want in your job, you should also think about your personal values and goals. How do you want to be remembered when you are gone? Did you ever notice that epitaphs do not include occupations, but instead focus on relationships? If a person was a physician, the epitaph might read "always helped others," or if a person was a lawyer it might read "brought justice to the world." What do you want people to write about you? Do you want your epitaph to say you worked hard for Company X, or instead inscribed a value or goal that you cared dearly about? Identifying your personal values and future goals can help you choose a job field or career.

Here are some goals based on personal values and the job or field they are related to:

Goals and Values	Job Field
Ensure all children can read	Education
Ensure the elderly have enough money to survive	Finance
Acquire special items for others	Real Estate; Personal Shopping; Antique Collector; Purchasing
Ensure fairness and justice prevails	Law; Public policy
Keep people healthy/fit	Athletics; Health Services; Alternative Medicine; Mental Health
Help people personally	Counseling; Caregiving; Teaching
Take care of animals or plants	Veterinary; Horticulture
Help others know God	Spiritual Advising

Can you make a match between your personal value or goal and the job field it's related to?

How do you want to be remembered? Write this personal value in the lines below and then add a possible career related to the value or goal:

Value:

_____

_____

Career:

_____

_____

STOP! **Add this personal value to your Profile at the end of the book. The career should be listed under "Careers to Explore."**

Incorporate Your Values into Your Career

Your values can have a profound effect on your career choice. If the career you choose conflicts with your values, your happiness and satisfaction working in this job may be in jeopardy. Making the right career choice to fit your values is extremely important.

Read the case study below to see how values can affect your career choices:

Midori's Dilemma

Midori has been out of the workforce for many years raising a family. Her last job was working as a biochemist for a small pharmaceutical laboratory. In this job she worked independently and alone in a quiet workplace, and created new technology. She received a high salary.

While her children were young, Midori was head of the school's Parent Teacher Association, Director of the Quilting Club where members work together on quilting projects, and was also the Events Coordinator for her neighborhood. She has loved her volunteer positions, but is now thinking of going back to work. Increasingly, she has valued working in a team on creative projects, helping the community and others, and likes an active environment, but her education and past career was in biochemistry.

Given these circumstances, write down how Midori's new values and past career might collide. What should she do?

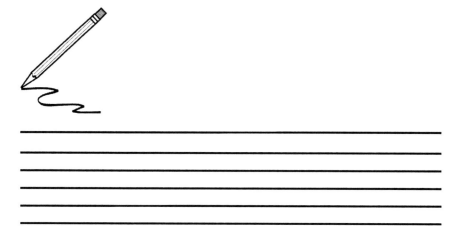

_____

_____
_____
_____
_____
_____

Our values make us unique individuals. We should always take our values into consideration as we make career choices. There may be a time when we have to compromise on some of our most important values. It will be important to recognize the one value we have chosen not to compromise when making a career decision or applying for a future job.

Chapter 3

Consider Your Interests

We choose our careers for a variety of reasons. One very compelling reason for choosing a career is interest in a particular occupation. Hopefully, you chose your current or past career because you were interested in it. It could be that you were artistic and wanted to work in an art museum, and or you loved the outdoors so you chose horticulture or wildlife management. You may have loved performing in front of an audience so you became a defense attorney, or you chose research because you were interested in discovering, collecting, and analyzing data.

What career, job, or volunteer position do you currently have?

_____

Do you have an interest in that field? If the answer yes, and you still love the career, consider a job in the same general field. If the answer is no, make it a goal to explore a few different careers as you work through this book.

John Holland, who created a career assessment called Self-Directed Search (see Chapter 10, Resources), has done extensive research on people who chose their careers based on their interests. His theory has been well documented and shows that people who are employed in the same types of work environments share many of the same interests. They chose their careers because of interest in the occupation. They also enjoy working with others who have the same interest.

If you ask people around you why they chose the career they are in, you would find that they might answer like this... "Well, I was very interested in..." So, it's very important to take your interests into account as you choose your career.

All Your Interests Count

Let's take a quick look at your personal interests, those things you do outside of work. What do you like to read or watch on television? What magazines do you read? What do you browse on the Internet? What are you favorite hobbies? Here are some topics:

Acting	Gardening
Artistic pursuits	Nursing
Building	Reading
Campaigning	Repairing
Designing	Sailing
Entertaining	Tutoring

Write your interests below. It doesn't matter how you picked up the knowledge, only that you love doing it.

_____

_____

_____

_____

_____

_____

STOP! **Add your top two personal interests to the Profile at the end of the book.**

Categorize your Interests

This next exercise explores your job interests. Think about how your interests may factor into your career decisions as you do this exercise.

In the categories listed below, circle the jobs that *most interest* you. Assume that all the jobs listed have equal pay and prestige associated with them.

#1 "INTERACTORS" (Interacts with things or the environment)

Athlete

Mechanic

Computer Technician

Electrician

Carpenter

Wilderness Expert

#2 "RESEARCHERS" (Explores and analyzes)

Researcher

Tax lawyer

Inventor

Investigator

Auditor

Scientist

#3 "CREATORS" (Creates unique work)

Artist

Writer

Composer

Designer

Performer

Musician

#4 "SOCIALIZERS" (Interacts with others)

Teacher

Caregiver

Mediator

Public Relations Specialist

Salesperson

Event Planner

#5 "CHALLENGERS" (Challenges others and/or the environment)

Leader

Adventurer

Entrepreneur

Director

Elected Official

Manager

#6 "ORGANIZERS" (Keeps things on time and in order)

Administrator

Collector

Organizer

Bookkeeper

Accountant

Production Associate

Next, look over your list and put a star next to the two categories that have the most words circled.

STOP! **On your Profile, write down the two categories you chose, plus any circled jobs that you would consider exploring for a future career.**

Matching Work Environments to Interests

In the list below, circle the two categories that you chose in the last exercise. Under that category, circle the work environments that most interest you.

#1 "INTERACTORS"

Work environment:

Independent	Hands-on approach
Results-oriented	Sports-related
Physical	Interaction with environment
Practical	Work with things instead of ideas
Action-oriented	

#2 "RESEARCHERS"

Work environment:

Independent	Technical
Curious	Flexible and unstructured
Problem-solving	Unconventional

Mathematical   Continuous learning

Scientific   Project- and task-oriented

#3 "CREATORS"

Work environment:

Independent   Imaginative

Expressive   Creative thinking

Non-conforming   Unstructured environment

Variety   Brainstorming opportunities

#4 "SOCIALIZERS"

Work environment:

Cooperative   Team-oriented

Friendly   Helping others

Interactive   Variety and action

#5 "CHALLENGERS"

Work environment:

Goal-oriented   Challenging

Flexible   Management opportunities

Independently owned business

Competitive/energetic environment

#6 "ORGANIZERS"

Work environments:

Indoor office environment   Administrative opportunities

Detail-oriented workplace   Efficient/well-run workplace

Larger, structured workplace

STOP! On your Profile, write down the circled work environments that most interest you.

Exploring your interests is an important part of getting to know yourself better. If you would like to obtain a more in-depth interest profile, take the Strong Interest Inventory or the Self-Directed Search (see Chapter 10, Resources).

If you are thinking about changing your career, be sure that you investigate the new career thoroughly and that you have an interest in it. When changing careers, you may need to build skills quickly. Interest in an occupation provides a stronger desire to learn a new skill, and you will most likely learn the skill more quickly because of your interest. In chapter four I'll focus on skills that you have, or need to acquire for a future career.

Find the passion. It takes great passion and great energy to do anything creative. I would go so far as to say you can't do it without that passion.

Agnes DeMille

What are you Passionate About?

The career you choose should not just fit your values and interests, it should also fulfill your passion. One of my objectives when exploring career options was to look for work where I could incorporate my passion. Many of you fell into your first job and may not have had much passion for the work you did. Or you may have been lucky, and come to love the work. Now that you are deliberately choosing a career, look for work that holds both your interest and passion. Both are possible if you keep an open mind and explore the careers that entice you.

To determine what type of work will give you a sense of satisfaction at the end of the day and one that you will be happy with at the end of the year, it's important to find work that is both interesting and fills you with passion. Are you passionate about something in your life now? Is this passion one that you would like to incorporate into a job for the next part of your life?

Think about things in your life that you love doing. It could be a hobby such as gardening or writing, a sport, a subject that you really enjoy like science or art history, a particular skill that you have, or a place that you love.

What are your passion(s)?

_____

_____

_____

_____

As you read this chapter, think about ways to incorporate passion into a career plan. Keep in mind that what you are passionate about today may change as you develop more interests and skills. Strive to find that place where work no longer feels like work.

So that you have an idea of how you can incorporate a hobby or activity into a new career, here are some jobs based on passion:

Your Passion: Photography

Commercial Photographer	Gallery Owner
Portrait Photographer	Medical Photographer
Graphic/Animation Designer	Layout Designer
Corporate Historian	Art Consultant
Advertising Assistant	Museum Curator

Your Passion: Sports

Sports Photographer	Sports Announcer
Sports Scout	Athletic Trainer
Recreation Director	Promotional Event Planner
Sports Agent	Sports Psychologist
Sports Therapist	Sporting Goods Salesperson

Your Passion: Computer Games

Software Designer/Tester	Software Engineer
Stage Technician	Toy Maker
Computer Animator	Graphic Design Engineer
Quality Engineer	Software Sales Rep

Your Passion: English

Journalist	Teacher/Professor
Television Producer	Technical Writer
Editor	Public Relations Director
Novelist/Poet	Lawyer
Communications Director	Broadcaster

Can you think of a job that would incorporate your passion? If so, write it below:

_____

_____

STOP! Add this to your Profile under "Careers to Explore."

In the next chapter I'll help you identify your current skills, and what skills you may need to build for a future career.

Chapter 4

Skills will lead the way

To get the job of your dreams, it's essential to complete a thorough inventory of your skills. You have been acquiring skills since childhood, and at each stage of your life, with practice and training, your skills have become more sophisticated. You listed many of your skills in Chapter 1. They are things like public speaking, building, writing, and communicating. You have skills that are core strengths, and also possess skills that you are still refining. As you move from job to job you bring many of your skills with you, enhancing and perfecting them over the years.

Transferable Skills vs. Technical Skills

In general, there are two types of skills – transferable skills and technical skills. The skills that provide you with the flexibility to work in many different settings are often called "transferable" skills. These skills can be used in multiple situations. They are the skills you want to build and perfect as you go through life. For example, in college you are assigned a presentation that requires research, graphic design, and the use of multimedia tools. Ten years later you may give a presentation to the board of directors of a corporation using these same skills at an expert level.

There are also job specific skills called "technical" skills. These skills are used for a particular job or workplace. They are not as easily transferred from job to job. An example of a technical skill is operating a cash register or finish carpentry. Most people will have a combination of both transferable and technical skills. This combination provides flexibility and opportunities in many different fields. In general, people will have many more transferable skills than technical skills. When you combine transferable and technical skills you create a well-balanced skill profile.

The chart below shows examples of both types of skills.

Technical Skills	Transferable Skills
Bookkeeping	Problem-Solving
Repairing computers	Writing
Using financial software	Teaching
Designing web pages	Selling
Operating ten key machine	Planning
Processing photos	Creating
Operating microscopes	Managing
Programming computers	Organizing

When you identify the skills you possess, you'll find you can use this knowledge in many ways. You can list your skills on a resume or cover letter, showing how your skills are the perfect fit for a particular job. When interviewing for a job, you can highlight the skills you have, communicating to the job recruiter how you have used these skills in the past and how they will benefit their company in the future.

Knowing your skills and strengths, what skills you like to use, and what skills you need to improve or learn are essential to future career building. You may discover that you have all the transferable skills you need for a career in a more enticing job field, and you have to acquire only a few technical skills in order to qualify for the job.

It's also important to know what skills you like to use and what you don't like, because nothing could be worse than starting a new job requiring the skills you don't enjoy using. This is a common trap. You get so good at a skill, and it's so easy for you to qualify for a job using that skill, that you fall right back into the same career, and quickly feel dissatisfied and unchallenged with the work. As you explore careers, focus on using your transferable skills in a different way. If there are skills that you are good at, but just don't want to use anymore, look for a career that does not use that skill in a primary job function.

It helps to know what skills you have so that you can easily choose a suitable job capitalizing on your strengths, and know exactly what skills you have to improve or acquire to obtain a future career. If you choose a career that enables you to use the skills you enjoy, you will learn the job more quickly, and your job satisfaction will be enhanced.

A Transferable Skills Example

Jochen likes to write, but doesn't know which direction he should choose to incorporate this skill into a future career. He realizes he has many job options, as shown in the following diagram. He can use his writing creatively, technically, in research, or investigation. His skill in writing is transferable to a variety of workplaces. His next step would be to explore the different careers more thoroughly. His final decision will include other things he has learned about himself, such as his interests and values.

Jochen's Career Options
Writing as a Transferable Skill

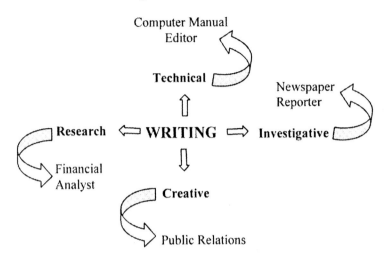

In the next exercise, you will be identifying and sorting your skills. You will identify transferable skills only. You do not need to use all of the skills listed, and you may add other skills you have in mind.

Identify Your Skills

Step #1   Read through each category of skills below.

Step #2   Each skill should be rated from 1 to 3:

3 = Skills I **perform well and like**. (You are very comfortable and confident using these skills.)
2 = skills **I have and like, but could improve**.
1= skills that I do NOT have but may want to **learn for a future career**.

Category 1: Communication Skills
(#1=low skill; #3=high skill)

____ **PERSUADE** - Convince others to change an attitude or take an action

____ **SELL** - Convince to make a purchase

____ **WRITE** - Demonstrate skill in use of language, grammar, and punctuation; edit

____ **ADVISE** - Give advice or opinions

____ **PUBLIC SPEAKING** - Enjoy speaking in front of small and large groups

____ **EXPLAIN** - Communicate a message or idea in a clear manner

____ **TEACH** - Help learn to do something

____ **NEGOTIATE** - Bring about an agreement

____ **LISTEN** - Focus carefully on verbal and nonverbal communication

____ **MEDIATE** - Resolve or settle differences between people

____ **COUNSEL** - Facilitate awareness of issues and provide guidance

____ _____(List additional communication skill)

How many core communication skills (marked #3) did you have? These are your communication strengths. ____

Category 2: Organizational Skills
(#1=low skill; #3=high skill)

____ **COORDINATE** - Arrange sequence and logistics of activities

____ **PRIORITIZE** - Set tasks based on urgency and importance

____ **ORGANIZE** - Pull things together in an orderly way

____ **SCHEDULE** - To plan ahead; organize events

____ **MONITOR** - Oversee and regulate flow of work

____ **FOLLOW THROUGH** - Ensure completion

____ **EXPEDITE** - Speed up results

____ **ADMINISTER** - To direct activities in a workplace

____**FILE** - To arrange for future reference

____ **PROCESS** - Follow method of doing something

____**RECONCILE** - Make accounts or ideas consistent

____ _____(List additional organizational skill)

How many core organizational skills (marked #3) did you have? These are your organizational strengths. _____

Category 3: Design/Creative Skills
(#1=low skill; #3=high skill)

____ **ILLUSTRATE** - To make clear using decorative drawings, designs

____ **CONSTRUCT** - Put together materials in creative way

____ **DEVELOP IDEAS** - Process information, looking at all possibilities

____ **INVENT -** To produce or create from imagination

____ **DESIGN** - Form a plan and carry it out

____ **COMPOSE -** Create musical or literary work

____ **INNOVATE -** Create new method of doing something

____ **CREATE -** Make or design

____**PERFORM -** Take part in musical program, play, or dance

____**PRODUCE** - Get a play, movie, program ready for presentation

____**DISPLAY -** Exhibit or present to others

____ _____ (List additional design/creative skill)

How many core design/creative skills (marked #3) did you have? These are your design/creative strengths. ____

Category 4: Problem-Solving Skills
(#1=low skill; #3=high skill)

____ **ANALYZE -** Examine in detail

____**PROBLEM SOLVE -** Explain or find a solution to a problem; resolve

____ **EVALUATE -** Assess needs/risks of a situation

_____**INTUITION** - Rely on insight beyond the senses; gut feeling

_____ **INVESTIGATE** - Seek out and study information

_____**ASSESS** - Estimate importance of something

_____ **REPAIR** - Put back in good condition

_____ **RESEARCH** - Investigate to discover facts, principles

_____ **DIAGNOSE** - Decide based on examination

_____ **ESTIMATE** - Calculate value, size, or cost

_____ **AUDIT** - Thoroughly examine and evaluate accounts or problems

_____ _____ (List additional problem solving skill)

How many core problem solving skills (marked #3) did you have? These are your problem solving strengths. ___

Category 5: Leadership Skills
(#1=low skill; #3=high skill)

_____ **ESTABLISH** - Set up business or plan

_____ **MANAGE** - Oversee policies and activities

_____ **BUDGET** - Plan and monitor expenditures

_____ **SUPERVISE** - Oversee workers or projects

_____ **INITIATE** - Take action without direction

_____ **LEAD** - Manage people; manage projects

____ **IMPLEMENT** - Take necessary steps towards goal

____ **CALCULATE** - Pay attention to detail; work with numbers

____ **MOTIVATE** - Organize people; inspire and stimulate to take action

____ **DECISION MAKING** - Choose the best option from alternatives

____ **TEAM BUILD** - Motivate and manage a group

____ _____ (List additional leadership skill)

How many core leadership skills (marked #3) did you have? These are your leadership strengths. _____

Use the next two pages to summarize your skills.

Skills I perform well and like (marked #3). **These are your core skills. Circle your five strongest skills.**

Skills I have and like, but could improve (marked #2).

Skills I might like to learn for a future career (marked #1).

Identify Skill Categories

The transferable skills you just evaluated are sorted into five categories. Sorting by category helps you get an idea of what types of skills you possess, or what types of skills you need to acquire. As an example, *persuade, sell,* and *explain* fall into the same category of skills – that of communication. Looking at your skills by category will help you quickly identify your overall strengths.

Five Skill Categories: 1. Communication Skills

2. Organizational Skills

3. Design/Creative Skills

4. Problem-Solving Skills

5. Leadership Skills

Let's look at how you rated your skills.

In the chart below, sort your skills by adding up how many skills were in each category.

Core skills: Skills that I like and perform well)	# of Skills (marked #3)
Communication Skills	
Organizational Skills	
Design/Creative Skills	
Problem-Solving Skills	
Leadership Skills	

Strongest Skill Categories: Looking at your core skills (those you perform well and like), which two categories (of the five categories: Communication, Organizational, Design/Creative, Problem-Solving, Leadership) have the largest number of skills? These are your strongest skill categories.

Category 1 _____

Category 2 _____

Skills I like, but could improve	# of Skills (marked #2)
Communication Skills	
Organizational Skills	
Design/Creative Skills	

Problem-Solving Skills	
Leadership Skills	

Which category needs improvement (category with the highest number)?

_____

Skills I would like to learn for my future career	**# of Skills (marked #1)**
Communication Skills	
Organizational Skills	
Design/Creative Skills	
Problem-Solving Skills	
Leadership Skills	

What skill category will you need to work on for a future career?

_____

Skills in the Workplace

Now that you have identified your own skills, think about matching your skills to workplace settings. Here are two examples of careers and different work environments for each one.

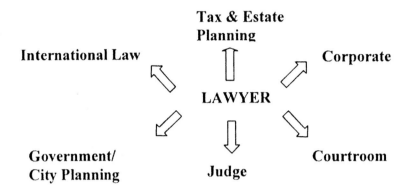

Which setting would emphasize speaking over writing?

_____

A lawyer can work in many different work settings, and a variety of skills may be needed. Remember that your skills and your goals may mesh nicely in one setting and totally clash in another setting.

The diagram below shows different workplaces for a teacher. Each setting may require different skills or use one skill more often.

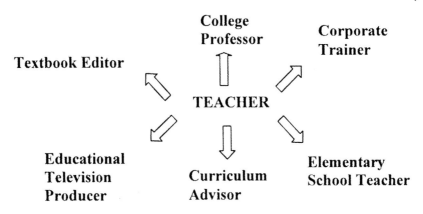

In what setting(s) would a teacher require more writing skills?

_____

Interest in a particular career, or a desire to use a particular skill can help you choose from the array of workplace settings for each field. Exploring the careers that interest you will also help you narrow down your options.

If you have previously explored some potential careers, which top skills (include your strongest skills and need to learn) will be most needed for this possible career?

As you plan your career, remember that there are always valuable skills to be learned no matter what you are participating in, whether it's volunteer work, sports, or your current job. Always work on building your skills. Skill building will enhance your options in the workplace at any stage in your life.

In this chapter you have identified your top five skills and your two strongest skill categories. You may have also identified some skills that you will need for a future career. Later in the chapter you will have the opportunity to set a goal to learn these new skills.

STOP! **Record your top five skills, two top skill categories and skills needed for a future career on your Profile**

Chapter 5

What's Your Style?

Working Style is Part of the Mix

I've had you look at your values, interests, and skills. Now it's time to look at your working style. We all have a working style or preference for how we perform on the job – how we interact with others and how we do our work. It's not a personality trait, it's more of a personal tendency or preferred style of working. In your past jobs you may have noticed how others focused on different aspects of the same job. One person may prefer focusing on details, one on the big picture. One person prefers working face to face and another prefers email.

People with different styles often prefer one type of career over another, but you will also find people with different styles in the same career. In fact, most teams have a mix of different styles. It's important to have work groups with different styles so that the group or team is efficient and effective. One style is not better than another, but employees that are flexible in their working style are often more valuable to the company than those who cannot adapt their style. After assessing your style, your goal should be to learn the styles of others, so you can be both flexible in your style and be able to relate more successfully with others as you work together.

The styles assessment below will help you identify your working style.

Style Assessment

Start by scoring each statement using this point system:

1 = Least like me
2 = Somewhat like me
3 = Most like me

I.	Point
Like facts and numbers	
Perfectionist	
Logical, reasonable	
Good analyzer	
Do things step by step	
Total Points:	

II.	Point
Sociable	
People-oriented	
Talkative	
Team-oriented	
Friendly	
Total Points:	

III.	Point
Look at the big picture (see cause and effect, future impact of actions)	
Visual	
Idea person	
Creative	
Imaginative	
Total Points:	

Each of the boxes above indicates a working style. Here are the three working styles:

Section I – Analyzer or Detail-Oriented
Section II – People-Oriented
Section III – Creative

Your **highest** score indicates your working style. If two of your scores were high, you should indicate both working styles. Which category or categories did you score the highest?

_____

_____

Your score may have indicated that you were a people-oriented person, an analyzer, creative, or a combination of two or even three (if you scored equally in each category).

If you scored over 12 or under 7 in any one category, you may want to work on one of the other categories to help you balance your working style. Being balanced or having strengths in two categories can help you be more adaptable in your work. It can also help you get the job of your choice, because more employers will want your skills.

Working Styles and Careers

You often find people with these working styles
in this type of job:

Analyzer

Database Administrator

Paralegal

Veterinarian

Data Analyst

Computer Engineer

Budget Analyst

Financial Analyst

Archivist

Accountant

Archeologist

Biologist

Stock Broker

Auto Mechanic

Chief Financial Officer

People-Oriented

Social Worker

Physician Assistant

Counselor

Health Information Technician

Physical Therapist

Clergy

Conservationist

Education Administrator

Customer Service Representative

Respiratory Therapist

Hotel Manager

Fundraiser

Human Resources Manager

Public Relations Representative

Creative

Desktop Publisher

Graphic Artist

Landscape Designer

Architect

Advertising Manager

Marketing Manager

Musician

Artist

Actor

Photographer

Museum Curator

Set Designer

Interior Decorator

Video Producer

Chef

Determining your working style can help you choose a career field. Some jobs require people skills, some require a high level of analytical skills, and some require creativity. Most jobs can be a blend of different styles, but this depends on the work location, work content, and relationships needed to do the job.

Many people score high in two areas. You can use this to your advantage. Most jobs have elements of two or even three working styles within them. For example, a technical writer might need to be both analytical and creative in order to write technical, precise text in a creative and interesting manner. A construction worker might need to be people-oriented and analytical in order to both work well with a client and to measure precisely. In fact, creativity may be needed in order to design a job that meets the demands of a client. A choreographer must be extremely creative, but also people-oriented in order to direct a cast.

Here are some jobs that typically require more than one working style (depending on the job description):

People-Oriented and Creative

Publicist

Training Specialist

Photojournalist

Choreographer

Buyer

Public Relations Manager

Teacher

Food Service Worker

Construction Worker

Occupational Therapist

Travel Agent

People-Oriented and Analytical

Dentist

Optician

Nurse

Reporter

Journalist

Dental Hygienist

Park Ranger

Sociologist

Computer Support Specialist

Police Officer

Physician

Lawyer

Emergency Medical Technician

Bank Officer

Creative and Analytical

Writer

Animator

Architect

Scientist

Archeologist

Engineer

There are many more careers that combine various working styles. Some of the careers listed, depending on the type of job, could also fit under another working styles. You can add many more jobs to these lists by thinking about what skills are needed for each job.

STOP! **On the Profile, write down your top working style(s).**

Satisfaction and Motivation

You should take into consideration your values, interests, skills, and working style when you choose your next career. Besides knowing your preferences and strengths in these areas, it's also important to know what motivates you to do your best in a job. If your next job does not include your identified motivators, your success in the workplace may be hampered and most certainly your level of satisfaction with the job will decrease.

Think about the jobs you have held in the past, both paid and unpaid. What factors kept you motivated to perform your best? What factors kept you happily engaged in the job? Circle the following words that motivate you to do your best work (choose all that apply):

I am motivated to do my best when I have:

Respect from colleagues	Challenging positions	Satisfaction with my job	Job pressure to perform
Approval from managers & others	Job security	Recognition for my contributions	Interest in my work
Non-monetary rewards	Opportunity to learn	High monetary compensation	Passion for the work
Pride in my work	Power to impact the workplace	Valued skills	Advancement opportunity

What are your top three motivators?

_____

_____

_____

STOP! **Add these motivators to your Profile.**

As you search for jobs, keep these motivators in mind. For example, if you feel money or other rewards are essential to keeping you motivated, be sure that your future job includes them. Maybe you need advancement opportunities or job security to feel satisfied. Be sure to get what you personally need as you choose a new occupation.

In addition to including motivators in your next job, also be sure that your job will be satisfying to you on a daily basis – that you really enjoy the work. You'll spend a large portion of your life working in the new career if you decide to work full time. How many hours a day, a week, and a year do you want to work? Know the optimal work schedule that suits you.

Be aware that there is not much time in a 24 hour day. You should decide how to spend your time. Here's a sample of how you may use one day if you work full time:

8-10 hours:
Full-time work

6-8 hours:
Sleep

6-10 hours left:
Eating, exercise, chores, commuting, family obligations, leisure, spirituality

Depending on where you live, type of commute, and the type of job you have (self-employed, union job, management, professional, or administrative position), your free time may be limited even more. If you don't care to work full time, consider the possibility of working part time. Is your chosen career flexible enough for you to choose less than full time work? Did you choose "Flexible Hours" as a top value? If so, research careers for part time work possibilities.

Having a job or career that is satisfying to you is important to your well being. Why work in a job you don't enjoy? Remember, you will spend a large portion of your life working if you choose full time work. Be sure that you've analyzed how much time you want to invest in your work, how much you have to work to meet your financial obligations, and if there are non-work activities that you want to include in your daily (or weekly) schedule. It may be that the weekends are dedicated to your other activities. That's fine, as long as you have looked at what you want and need, and that you create a balanced life for yourself.

Ideal Workplace Schedule

Think about the way you currently work. Don't take into consideration whether the work is paid or unpaid. Do you like your work schedule? Do you get enough time off to pursue other interests? Is your schedule flexible and unstructured, or regimented? What schedule suits you the best?

Check the ideal workplace schedule(s) that you would most enjoy (assume that you love your new career):

❑   Work 8 hours per day with lunch break
❑   Work a split shift (2-4 hours off between work periods)
❑   Work 10 hours per day, 4 days a week
❑   Work Part-time (30 hours or less)
❑   Other daily/weekly schedule:
_____

❑   Summers off
❑   Time off to attend to personal/family matters
❑   How much vacation would suit you? _____days/weeks
❑   Other time off schedule:
_____

Knowing the workplace schedule that you would most enjoy will help you choose a career. This isn't to say that the career you choose will accommodate your ideal schedule, only that some careers are more conducive to having a flexible schedule, while other workplace schedules can be negotiated with a manager. Knowing what you prefer is the first step in getting a schedule that fits you the best.

STOP! **Add your ideal schedule to the Profile at the end of the book.**

Chapter 6

Mix and Match: Find your Patterns

In the last five chapters I've helped you focus on getting to know yourself better. Your next big step is career exploration. You may be asking "What careers should I explore?" If you have no idea, now is the time to look at your Career Profile. Examining the "mix" of answers on your Profile and then "matching" these to potential careers is a crucial step. In this chapter you will examine your Profile, but before you choose careers based on your Profile, take a moment to look back at how you chose your current or last career.

Circumstance and Careers

In your current or last career did you "fall" into the job or was it a planned experience? Very often a person goes from job to job, or career to career without consciously considering the future or without looking at or matching their values, interests, skills, passions, and working style to the potential career. Often circumstances beyond your control affected your career choice. For example you were laid off and had to find a new job quickly – any job. Or your funding for college disappeared and you were plunged into the workplace. Or a chance encounter led you to career that you hadn't previously considered. Maybe you just took a job because it sounded like a good one. For all your "planned" efforts, circumstances may have sidetracked your chosen career path. There's a good chance that this will happen to you again. This isn't always a bad thing and may indeed be a fortuitous event. The consequences of a circumstance can set you back in your career or lead you to unexpected success.

For example, Sally Ride couldn't decide between two careers: scientist or tennis pro. She eventually chose scientist – studying laser physics and X-ray astrophysics – a path leading to teaching and research in an academic environment. One day she saw a newspaper ad. NASA wanted scientists to join the space program as astronauts. The rest was history when in 1983, she became the first U.S. woman astronaut to orbit the Earth.

This goes to show that no matter how you plan, circumstances can change the path you are currently going down – with astonishing results!

The late John Gardner, former Secretary of Health, Education, and Welfare and Founder of Common Cause had this to say about his career:

My career had all the straight-line consistency of a tangled ball of yarn. Did I know where I was headed? Absolutely not! Did I plan my career moves in a logical progression? Absolutely not. There was no grand design. I was a California boy, stumbling cheerfully through life, succeeding, falling on my face, picking myself up and plunging ahead, holding onto some simple values, trying to live with a civil heart as someone said, always learning, always trying, always wondering.

There may have been a time in your life when things didn't go the way you would have liked, or an event took an unexpected turn that led you down an unplanned path. Unexpected circumstances have a way of popping up when you least expect them. The key to success is making these circumstances work for you. Seize the moment and think about positive outcomes and future opportunities. And if things still don't work out for a chosen career, have a contingency plan:

- Keep your eyes open for an alternative career path.
- Brush up on unused skills so that you can change jobs quickly.
- Revive a past interest that could lead to an alternative career.
- Keep in contact with those who can help you get the job you really want.
- Explore night classes at a local college.
- Network with your clients about careers.

- Visit the chamber of commerce to learn more about other businesses in your area.
- Volunteer.
- Continue to explore other career and educational options.
- Learn as much as you can on the job.
- Set short-term and long-term goals.

Were your past (or current) careers planned or did you "fall" from one job to the next?

_____

_____

_____

Finding Patterns for Success

Analyzing your Career Profile will help you know yourself better and help you discover career options to explore. Take time now to review each section of your Profile, looking for logical patterns.

- Is there something on your Profile that you have repeated over and over? Look for words and phrases that go together, complement each other, or even overlap.

- Look closely at your accomplishments. Are there skills and interests embedded in the statements that you could use to establish additional patterns?

- Does your life goal mesh with your interests?

Here's an example of a pattern: you notice that you are people-oriented (your working style), a socializer (your interest), and like working as part of a team (your value). You would write this pattern down on the lines below. You may see multiple patterns. If so, write them down. **Your goal is to match your patterns with possible careers.**

If you have difficulty, ask someone close to you to review your profile and help you identify your patterns. You could ask a family member, friend, or someone you work with. If you wish, a career counselor can help you analyze the information. Career counselors can be found at career centers across the country. Consult your local phone directory or use online resources.

My Career Profile Patterns:

_____

_____

_____

_____

The patterns you have noted will help you to narrow down your options in order to conduct a more focused and successful career search.

Choosing Careers to Explore

The careers you choose to explore should be based on the patterns you see in your Career Profile, including your interests, skills you want to use in the future, your passion, life goals, and even desired work schedules. What careers are already on your Profile? What other careers would you consider? What job options or potential careers would fit your Profile? What job would use your passions and interest in a satisfying way? Here are some other ways to find out about different careers that fit your Profile:

- Search the online *O*NET* (See Resources, Chapter 10). Enter your skills and see what jobs match your skills.
- Read books on new jobs and careers and see what patterns in your profile match the career.
- Look for jobs using your passion or interest and see what skills and education are needed for the job.
- Try an online in-depth assessment (see Resources) to help you identify specific careers that fit your interests.

If you find a career that uses your strengths, but you no longer wish to use these skills, an alternative career choice would be wise. Also, be sure to take into consideration where you want to work. Are you willing to relocate? Some jobs can only be performed in specific geographical regions. For example, a ski instructor typically works at a ski area in the mountains. Do not take into consideration the salary level of the job at this time. Just work on putting together a list of careers to explore.

Alice's Profile

Life Goal	To maintain my health, have time to spend with family and friends, and to travel.
Values	Flexible hours; Working as part of a team; Outdoor workplace; Make independent decisions
Interests/ Environments	Socializer, Creator Friendly, Variety and action; Creative thinking; Physical

Skill Categories	
	Communication, Design/Creative
Working Style	People-oriented and Creative
Motivation	Recognition for my contributions, Passion for work, Non-monetary Reward
Passion	Travel and photography

Alice's next step would be to take all of this information, and see if there is a pattern. She noticed that she wanted flexible work that involved people and creativity. She wanted to make her own decisions and preferred an outdoor or physical job. She also hoped to use her passion for travel or photography. She chose to look in the *Dictionary of Occupational Titles* (DOT) and *O*NET* for careers with that focus. She read *Popular Photograph* and *Travel* magazines, and books on travel writing careers. She also researched sites on the Internet that had to do with travel jobs, freelance jobs, photography careers, and teaching adventure classes.

Here are the career options she chose: photojournalist, adventure travel guide, experiential learning instructor, Outward Bound instructor, travel agent, writer of travel books and articles, photographer.

Her next step would be to research each career in-depth and narrow down her career options.

Note: It is important to have more than one career option. There are thousands of occupations to explore, and new jobs are being developed every year. If you need more career ideas, ask someone close to you to identify jobs that they feel would ideally suit you. Or find a mentor or a career counselor to guide you.

List your career options here:

_____

_____

_____

_____

Exploring Your Career Options

Next, spend some time researching and exploring your career options. Your research can include:

- Exploring the *Occupational Outlook Handbook, Dictionary of Occupational Titles* (DOT), or the online *O*NET* (which also lists careers and skills needed)
- Reading books and magazine articles
- Volunteering at conventions of interest
- Using the Internet resources in Chapter 10
- Researching programs at colleges and universities
- Looking up salary ranges on the Internet

The O*NET is an excellent resource for exploring careers. You can also use the Internet as an exploration tool. For example, if you want to find out more information about sports agents, use an Internet search engine to look for key words such as sports agent job, sports agent salary, or sports agent career; or look for books such as *50 Cool Jobs in Sports* or *Career Opportunities in the Sports Industries*.

In the next chapter, you will learn to conduct informational interviews – an essential tool in career exploration. Informational interviews will provide you with specific information on the careers that you have chosen to explore.

STOP! **Add the careers that interest you to your Career Profile.**

Is it a Match?

When you put your Profile side by side with the careers you gathered, in some cases they will match very neatly and in others they will not. It is important to recognize when a choice is NOT a good fit. For example, you may think you want to be a nurse, but you've discovered that you are not people-oriented and you don't like science. In this case, a career in nursing may not be in your best interest. Be sure to take careers off your list that do not mesh with your profile. Expand your career search if necessary.

And If All Else Fails...

Life will not always be predictable and sometimes the best plan will not take shape easily. Circumstance or serendipitous experiences may determine your career choice. Embrace circumstance as a reason to seize an opportunity. A mentor may come into your life at a time when you are making a career decision, or you might unexpectedly meet someone who works in a field that fascinates you, or you may face a personal setback that will change your plans. Whatever the reason, recognize these as learning experiences. Your dream job is truly just around the corner.

Chapter 7

Connect For Success

I've found that connecting with others is an effective way to both learn about potential careers and search for a job. One way to connect with others and quickly learn about a career that interests you is to conduct informational interviews.

Informational Interviews for Career Exploration

Information is the key to success. Whether you're writing a research proposal or planning your own future, the more information you obtain, the better the outcome. The most honest and informative information on careers generally comes from people in the workplace.

The purpose of the informational interview is to obtain the information that you need in order to choose the right career. An informational interview is NOT a job interview. It is NOT a time to ask for a job. However, it is a great opportunity to explore a work environment you are interested in. You are the interviewer! Informational interviews are helpful in the following ways:

- Meet people with experience in a career field.
- Learn what skills and education you may need to be successful in the field.
- Learn more about an industry, company, or workplace.
- Observe the work environment.
- Research career options.
- Receive feedback on your career plan.
- Develop your interviewing skills.
- Determine if your career choice is realistic and obtainable.
- Benefits both parties – it's possible that you have information about the company that they did not know about.

• Establishes a relationship.

Who should you interview?

First choose the career field or company that interests you.

Then make a list of people whom you know: family, friends, counselors, and relatives. Many of these people will be able to provide you with referrals. Ask them, *"Do you know anyone I can talk to regarding this career or field?"* Also search the internet to access companies, associations, conventions, career networks, and organizations. Many times conventions will need local volunteers. Use these resources to make your initial contacts. If you are reluctant to call for an interview, you may introduce yourself by letter first, stating that you will follow-up with a phone call.

Practicing for an informational interview is important. It will help you perfect your communication skills and enable you to test your interview questions on people you know prior to the actual event.

You may also have an unplanned opportunity to conduct an informational interview on an airplane, standing in line at a movie, or at a department store counter. Wherever and whenever you conduct your informational interview, follow these six guidelines to ensure success.

1. Schedule the interview

Informational interviews are short meetings (30 minutes maximum) at a mutually agreed upon time. It is to your advantage to schedule the meeting at the person's place of employment. Introduce yourself as someone wanting information and guidance because you are interested in that career. It is usually easier to arrange an interview when you have a referral. Be aware that many people have busy schedules, so call or e-mail to schedule an interview when it is most convenient to the person being interviewed. Most people will be happy to discuss their career path, but if you do not get a response, it usually means the person you contacted is just too busy.

2. Prepare for the interview

It is important that you prepare ahead of time. Know something about the person's career field and the company. Information can be obtained from the human resources department, your local public library, and sometimes on the Internet. Prepare a list of questions that are important to you. Here are some sample questions:

Tell me about your career path.
Did you plan to have this career?
How do you spend a typical day?
What types of people do you work with?
What do you like or dislike about your job?
What type of education do you need for your position?
What are the top five skills you need in this career?
What part of your job is the most challenging?
Can you advance from this job? In this career?
What is the salary range?
Do you see your field changing in the future?
Do you think your job will still be here in 20 years?
What career planning suggestions do you have for me?
Do you have any other suggestions to help me obtain more information?
Could you refer me to someone else in your field?

If you do not have the requirements for the job (i.e. five years experience, advanced degree) and wonder if the requirement is essential, ask: Do you know anyone who got this job without the experience or requirements that you outlined? How can I reach that person?

3. Begin the interview

Remember to arrive at least 10 minutes early for your interview. Relax and observe your surroundings. Dress the same way you would dress for a job interview. Shake hands and thank him or her for taking the time to meet with you. Smile and try to be enthusiastic. As you ask questions, try to maintain eye contact as much as possible while jotting down notes.

4. Gain information from the interview

Your initial question should be one that helps you get to know the person. You may want to choose *"Tell me about your career background"* or *"Tell me about your career path"* as your first question. Make sure you allow the person you are interviewing be the expert. You are there to listen and learn. Remember to ask your most important questions first, since you have a limited amount of time.

5. Conclude the interview

At the end of the interview it is appropriate to ask for additional names of people who may be able to help you. If the person you just interviewed doesn't have the type of job you're interested in, he or she may know someone who has a job more in line with your career goal. Make sure to thank your interviewee sincerely for his or her time and guidance.

Before you leave, ask for a business card, so you have the correct spelling and address for a thank-you note.

6. After the interview

The thank-you letter should be sent within the first few days after your interview. Here's a sample thank-you note to get you started.

Date:
Person's Name:
Title:
Company Name:
Address:

Dear Mr./Ms._____,

Thank you for _____(time, valuable information, clarification, encouragement, guidance and thoughtfulness). I was really impressed by _____ (mention something that stood out for you during the interview).

Thank you for _____ (any names this person gave you and when you will contact them). I plan to _____(What will you do next?)

Sincerely,

Your Name

After completing your informational interview, you will have gained first-hand information about a career. Use this information to help you make a decision about pursuing that particular field or company. You might also want to think about the top five skills needed for the job. Compare these with the skills you listed on your Career Profile. Is this the type of workplace that suits you? What else might you need to get started in this field? Do you need specific training for the job?

Connections: Communicating Effectively

I've also discovered that by connecting with others and effectively communicating, you will not only be able to quickly learn about a career that interests you, but also expand your job search so that you have many people working to help you find the job of your dreams.

Effective communication means:

- focusing your entire attention on the person.
- being involved. Use your body position (i.e. lean forward, be open) to encourage the speaker and signal your interest.
- setting aside your prejudices and opinions.
- refraining from interrupting the speaker.
- focusing on the communication style of others (verbal and nonverbal) by adapting your own style
- being aware. Nonverbally acknowledge points as you listen to the speaker.
- restating and summarizing key points after listening.

Effective communication is important in every job, especially in this day and age. Our country has shifted from manufacturing as our primary business to providing knowledge and services to people around the globe. For a company or organization to be successful in providing services to people, it has to listen to what people want, fulfill their needs, and supply ongoing support. This means that good communication skills are essential for career success.

The Value of Networking

Communicating with others who can help you with your career is often called "networking." Establishing a network of friends, family, colleagues, neighbors, and acquaintances that in turn tap their networks can pay off handsomely when launching your job search. In fact, 65 - 70% of those in the workforce got their jobs as a result of their network. As you actively promote yourself to others, consider everyone you talk to as a possible source of information, or someone who may talk to others about your career and job preferences. Develop a list of contacts and expand your list each day. Add to your list as you attend meetings, workshops, and lectures. Start keeping a list of names and contact information now. Don't start the list after you've left a job or were laid off. Remember that just one chance conversation with one person on your list or someone you met at a party could help you learn more about a job or even get you a job interview.

On the lines below, start your networking list. Write down the names of the top ten people you will contact regarding a career(s) that you are interested in:

- _____
- _____
- _____
- _____
- _____
- _____
- _____
- _____
- _____
- _____

Keep a list of contacts and add to them. Many people keep a contact list of over 200 names. You can, too. Your network will help you find people to talk to. With your active network and personal research you should be very successful identifying appropriate career options and finding a job that best suits you.

Choosing a career requires a lot of time and energy. If you are a good communicator, you can use your time wisely and obtain knowledge that you will never find in any career book. Listening carefully is important for informational interviews. Most people love to talk about themselves, so it's usually very easy to obtain information about their jobs. Listen for positive and negative comments and assess their importance in relation to your career goals. What may be a negative for one person in his or her job may be a positive for you.

There are also a couple of other people who can help you with your careers search – a mentor or a career counselor.

Find a Mentor

Studies have shown that being mentored is directly linked with academic and professional success.

Why find a mentor?

There are many reasons to seek out a mentor. The most compelling reason is that it's extremely helpful to have someone who knows you and believes in you, to guide you in your learning. Mentors provide an opportunity for you to learn new skills and gain access to people and workplaces that would otherwise take years to find. You can obtain insight from an experienced individual who shares your passion, and who can advise and encourage you when you have to make career choices or life decisions. You can set up a mentoring situation in many ways – face to face, by telephone, e-mail or by mail – whichever is preferable to each of you.

Who should you choose for a mentor?

Sometimes mentors are right under your nose and you don't realize it. Think of people in your life who would make good mentors.

- Colleagues or someone in your workplace
- Someone in the field or career that interests you
- Friends

- Alumni of your alma mater
- Speakers at a professional conference
- Authors of books you admire
- Counselors
- Community officials
- Local college mentor services
- Local chamber of commerce members

Contact one of these potential mentors and establish a relationship. You can start by phoning or writing a potential mentor requesting only a minute or two of their time. You may ask them to answer a specific question or recommend a class or seminar. You may even have information that can help them. Slowly build the relationship. You don't have to settle for just one mentor. You can have many mentors that you call on for different types of information. Be sure to thank your mentor and keep them up to date on your progress.

Where else can you find a mentor?

There are a number of other places to find a mentor:

- Check internet sites for mentor services and organizations.
- Scan the trade publications associated with your desired field at the local library and identify mentors from biographical articles or topic areas.
- Place an ad on an internet site requesting a mentor in your area.
- Find businesses on the internet that reflect your interest area and contact them by e-mail to see if they have mentors available.
- Visit a senior center and let them know you are looking for mentor in a specific area.

Write your potential mentor's name here:

_____

Using a Career Counselor

If you want more career help, there are community career centers, community college career centers, private centers and career counselors in private practice. Here are some guidelines for choosing a career counselor:

- Always ask to see a person's credentials.
- Find another counselor if he or she seems overly concerned about fees.
- Do not sign any up-front contracts.
- Be concerned if you are bombarded by requests for costly testing.
- Ask yourself if you communicate well with the counselor (Is he or she a good listener?).
- Be sure you understand what the counselor has to offer you (i.e., resume writing or counseling).

During your counseling session remember that:

- Testing (assessments) can be useful to initiate a valuable discussion with a career counselor, but it's up to you to provide as much information as you can in order to achieve your goal.

- Sometimes, just hearing it from others is validation that you are on the right track and that's what you needed the most (the "Aha, I knew that all along!" reaction).

Communication is an important part of the career self-management process. Listen to others, but also remember to listen to yourself. You know yourself best, so don't be pushed into a career that you don't really like (but were afraid to say). Keep all comments and feedback in perspective.

STOP! **Take time to research your career options thoroughly and narrow down your choices.**

Chapter 8

Dilemmas, Decisions, and Goals

By now you've chosen a number of career options and explored careers that interested you. Before making a final choice of a career there are two more things you should consider – your financial situation and an alternative nontraditional working option such as starting your own business.

Can You Afford It?

Before you make a final career choice, consider the financial impact of taking a job in the career fields that you have chosen.

- Will the new career fit your current lifestyle both financially and personally?
- Can you afford to change careers right now?
- Do you have children in school who need your financial support?
- Does your spouse or partner work, and is he or she willing to provide financial support as you establish a new career?
- If you don't have a partner, do you have the financial means to change your career?
- Do you have sufficient retirement income and savings to achieve your goals?

Analyze the following three items carefully and in-depth on a separate sheet of paper:

- What will be your new projected income?

- What is your present budget?

- What is your projected budget?

- Is there a difference and what will you do about it?

Note: Be sure to provide for other factors such as health insurance, investments, retirement funds, estate planning, and children's college funds.

Analyze your figures, assess the impact on your pocketbook, then either go with your plan or revise it. If appropriate, consider how much time it will take before your salary is high enough to make ends meet.

Maybe you don't currently work, and won't need the extra income. Then this scenario would leave you the flexibility to choose a career for passion. For example, you love golf and skiing and will retire with good retirement benefits in one year. You just need a little bit of extra cash to meet your needs. Consider a job that may be low paying, but may also be stress free. You might work at a golf course or a ski area. Or if you love to travel, become a flight attendant or courier. Maybe you want to travel and help people, consider the Peace Corps.

Start Your Own Business

I've found that an alternative to working for others is to start your own business, as I did. Prior to starting a business, read everything you can on the subject. Research business startups thoroughly, and interview those who have done it and have been successful. Also interview those who did not succeed to get a good idea of what could go wrong. Unless you are willing to put everything at risk and can afford it, don't quit your day job.

❏ What kind of business are you thinking about? Is it a business you already know thoroughly? For example, you work in an Information Technology department and want to freelance as a software programmer. Or are you thinking about a new field? For example, you want to become a writer, sell clothing, or you have invented a device that you want to sell.

90

❑ Discuss the idea with your spouse, partner, and/or a close friend.

❑ Do your homework. Research the specific market. Interview those who are in that particular business. Focus on interviewing business owners farther from your home so that you don't compete with their business. They'll be more apt to give you information.

❑ Last, consider if you want to work in a home office or distant office. If it's at home, be aware that you may feel isolated. Does this work for you or are you someone who needs a busy office environment?

❑ Know yourself – your values, preferences, work environment, and motivation to see if it fits with your business plan.

❑ And again, research, research, research. Talk to those who have both succeeded and failed.

After you considered your financial situation, narrow down your career choices. In the following section you will be making some final career decisions based on the information you have gathered.

Make a Decision

By this time, you may be saying to yourself "Now what do I do, I have so many career options to choose from?"

Decision-making is a part of the career process. This may mean narrowing down the career choices, choosing the right goals, and/or choosing the right direction with regard to career and educational options. It means choosing a direction when there is a fork in the road. Up until now, you've spent most of the your time exploring your options. You may ask yourself, *"What happens if I don't make the right decision?"*

Instead ask:

"What is the worst thing that can happen if I make the wrong decision?"

Something that I've learned is that you can't get it wrong! If you can live with the outcome, then you can face the fear of making the wrong decision. Most people who make the wrong career decision will generally say that it may have been the wrong decision, but it was an important learning experience. Sometimes the wrong decisions also lead us to alternative careers that weren't considered before.

Here's how to make a good career decision

1. Use Information: Gather all of the information you can before making a decision.

2. Be Realistic: Will it really work for me? Am I looking at all aspects of the situation? Is this career feasible for where I am in my life now?

3. Be Flexible: Leave some room for flexibility in your decision-making process. Have a contingency plan. If all else fails, what is your next best choice?

Use the worksheet below to help you make a decision on your career options.

Steps for Making Good Decisions

1. I would like to make a decision regarding the following:

2. What options am I considering?
a.

b.

3. What general factors do I want to consider? (For example, the job must use what specific values, interests, skills or working styles for me to be happy.)

4.   Which factors, if not met, will cause one option to fail? (For example, the job must use a particular value or I won't consider the career.)

5.   Compare the options using a pro and con list. Jot down the positive things that could happen (Pro) and the negative aspects (Con) of each option:

Option 1   Pro   Con

Option 2   Pro   Con

6.   Evaluate the results. Which option best meets my requirements?

Ask for help from others if necessary.

Set Your Goals

Now you are ready to set some goals! It's important to establish goals so that you know where you are going and how to get there. Studies have repeatedly shown that individuals who verbally communicate goals to others are more likely to achieve their goals. Those who also write down their goals are even more successful in achieving them.

Setting goals enables you to take action. Many times there are so many possibilities that it's hard to sort out what you really want. Setting a goal, even a small one, will help you take steps towards a realistic and meaningful career.

Think about three things you need to do to pursue your desired career, or to just get started moving in that direction. The items you choose may be related to the education you need for the job, further exploration of potential careers or jobs, interviewing those with a position you seek, or even getting a part time job in the desired field.

What are the three things you need to do to get started pursuing your desired career?

1. _____
2. _____
3. _____

Goal setting is a flexible process: Goals are meant to change as you grow and change. Many people shy away from setting goals because they have not had success in achieving their goals. Remember to be realistic in setting goals for yourself. Ask yourself how motivated you were to actually achieve a desired goal in the past. The success in goal setting depends on your honest assessment and realistic expectations in making the goal come true.

Let's review Stefan's Career Profile. What will his next steps be?

Stefan's Career Profile

Life Goals	To establish a successful business that would satisfy my need for autonomy and independence in my work
Values	Flexible hours, challenging work, independent decision making
Personal Interests	Long distance biking
Interests/Work Environments	Socializer, challenger, independent, results-oriented, variety and action, communicator
Skill Categories	Leadership skills, organizational skills
Working Style	Analytical, people-oriented
Motivation	Challenging position, passion for the work, power to impact the workplace
Passion	Connoisseur of fine wines
Career Options	Wine tour business owner; Vineyard owner/operator; Active travel business manager or events/research coordinator; Bike shop business owner or manager

Next, Stefan explored his career interests, comparing what types of skills, work environments, and values were needed for each career, and then validated this with his life goals. He made an appointment with someone who worked in each field, asking them about their job. He decided that starting a wine tour business would give him the most satisfaction.

He then formulated two long-term goals: Open a wine tour business within one year; explore the options of developing the business for active travel, specifically bike tours through the wine country.

He also made plans for two short-term goals related to his goals:
- Research the tour market business in-depth, determining viability of the business in this region.
- Put together a business plan with financing options.

STOP! **Take a few minutes to review your Career Profile. Identify at least one long-term goal to use in the following Goal Setting Worksheet. Keep these points in mind:**

- Set realistic goals with realistic time frames.

- Create long-term goals, short-term goals, and action steps.

- For each long-term goal, make a list of all of the tasks that you should do to achieve the goal. These tasks should be listed as short-term goals or action steps.

- Set aside and schedule the time to accomplish your tasks.

- Solicit support from others in reaching your goals.

- Reward yourself for accomplishments. Acknowledge all steps, no matter how small.

It's your turn to set some goals!

Goal-Setting Worksheet

Choose one career goal. Decide whether it is a **Long-Term Goal**, a **Short-Term Goal**, or an **Action Step**. Enter goals and action steps in the appropriate boxes.

Long-Term Goals (2-10 years) – General statements describing your career destination
Short-Term Goals (6 months - 1 year) – Specific actions leading to your long-term goals
Action Steps (1 month) – Very specific behaviors leading toward your short-term goals

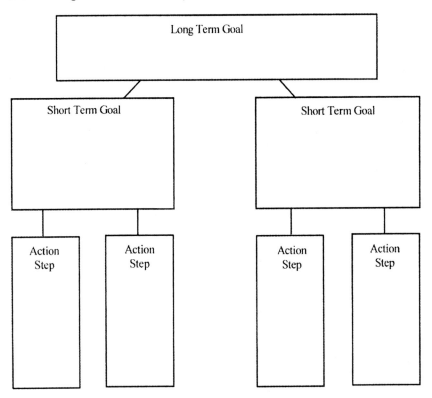

STOP! **List your long-term and short-term goals on the Career Profile. Take action now by pursuing the goals you have listed.**

Using your Career Profile in the future

Now that you know how to put together a Career Profile, you can use these skills throughout your life. Refer back to your Career Profile often to reassess or reaffirm your skills, values, interests, and goals. Don't forget that your passion is also important!

Remember, when you reach a fork in the road you will need to make a decision on which way to go and then set goals to get there. Having written goals provides you with a powerful tool to help you obtain what you desire. Read them daily! Before you know it, you will have reached your goals!

Chapter 9

Take it From Here

By now, you know yourself quite well – your values, interests, skills, working style, and passion. You've explored careers, evaluated your choices and set some goals. If you are ready for that job, it's time to plan a well-organized job search.

The Job Search

The perfect job for you is just around the corner. All you have to do is find it. Here are the general steps you should take to be successful in your search:

1. Find out what jobs are out there

- Check the job postings in your field of interest
- Read want ads in newspapers and other publications
- Search the internet (see Chapter 10, Resources)
- Talk to everyone on your networking list

2. Target choice employers using written and in-person methods

- Correspond directly with an employer via letter, email, or phone
- Develop specialized position proposals to potential employers if you are interested in creating your own job
- Follow-up by telephone to postings, ads, job listings
- Attend events (conferences, job fairs, etc.)
- Hold networking chats by email, phone, or in person

3. Prepare your resume and cover letter (tailored to each job), and practice interviewing for the job

Steps to Take When Jobs are Scarce

What if the economy is bad, there is a high unemployment rate, or there are only a few jobs available in your chosen field? Remember that you can always get a job, it just might take more time and effort on your part. You must also have top skills for the job, be realistic about your chances of obtaining the job, or you may have to adjust your goals to fit the economic reality. Here are some steps to help you when the job market is bleak:

- Network! Call 50 or 100 people who like you and let them know what kind of job you are looking for.

- Look in the want ads. When applying, explain how you meet all the requirements in the ad. For salary requirements, answer "flexible."

- Send emails to actual people (not just the Human Resources department), and follow-up with a phone call. Get contact names off the internet, from others, or call the company. Send 50 or more emails!

- If there aren't many jobs available in your field, expand your search. Look at other geographical areas if moving is an option (or propose working via telecommuting), check both local and national journals, and attend conferences and other events.

- Last, don't take a month to do this – get it all done in a few weeks. That way any response you get will provide encouragement to keep looking and you might just get a job offer right away!

Putting this much effort into a job search is sure to get you an interview for a choice job, as long as your resume and cover letter are superb, and you are qualified for the job. If you still have problems finding the perfect job, revisit your goals. Are you being realistic with regard to your qualifications (do you need more education or training)? Does the job your want even exist (can you create it, starting your own business)? Are you willing to move to get a job that only exists in specific locations (if not, reconsider your choice of careers)? Keeping an open mind with regard to the job possibilities, and being flexible when alternative job options come up will bring you more success. Don't narrow your focus ("I want only that one job.")

Commit yourself to these steps for a well-planned job search:

1. When will you start your job search?

2. Who will you involve? Include when and how (letters, email, phone)

3. When will you complete your resume?

As you go about your job search, you must:
❑ Research new jobs
❑ Conduct informational interviews
❑ Make new job contacts

❑ Follow up on leads
❑ Sent out resumes and fill out job applications

4. When do you expect your job to begin?

Write Your Resume

Start by gathering your old resumes from previous jobs and information about the job you are applying for. Decide on the type of resume you should write for the job. There are a number of different types of resumes you can write, and many books available in bookstores and the library on how to write them. Be sure to look at different examples before you write your own, including the examples in this book.

The three basic types of resumes covered in this book are:

• Chronological resumes - this resume presents information in chronological order, with education and employment dates reversed (current or most recent information first). It lists employment history including functions of the job in one category, usually called "Experience."

• Functional resumes - this resume emphasizes abilities and qualifications. It lists functions of the job in a separate category, and has a separate employment history category listing only place and dates. Have a good reason for using this type of resume. It is commonly used when you want to change your career direction, re-enter the workplace, or you have employment gaps. A person using this resume may not have the work history to support the qualifications of the job (but have the skills needed for the job).

• Combination resume - similar to the chronological resume, but also includes a quick synopsis of your skills (a "Skill Summary"), highlighting your value to the employer

Consider your own qualifications for the job, and job history before deciding which type of resume to use. A good compromise would be the combination resume. You could tailor the skills summary category to highlight the skills that best qualify you for the job.

Remember that the purpose of a resume is to get you an interview. The resume is the first impression an employer will have of you, so it is important to present yourself in a way that will make the employer want to talk to you in person.

When you begin to write your resume, use the following guidelines:

• Your resume should be no more than two pages.
• Use good quality white or light-colored paper with matching envelopes.
• Place your name at the top of the page.
• Describe your experience with specific skills, accomplishments, and education.
• Lay out your resume so it is easy to read (no columns, italics, shadows, underlines etc.).
• Check spelling and punctuation carefully.
• Have at least two people proofread it.
• Use standard fonts.
• Use a font size between 10 and 14.

Most large companies and organizations will scan your resume and place it in their computer database. A smaller company or organization will ask the hiring manager to read your resume. Regardless of whether a computer or a person first reads your resume, you will need to write it a similar way.

In A Scanner Friendly Resume:

- You should include the most likely keywords or phrases for the job. The recruiting software that the employer uses will search for resumes with specific words or phrases related to the job. Typically, these words have to do with skills, abilities and competencies.

- You should use keywords from job postings and advertisements. There are thousands of keywords out there, and all are specific to the job. Here are the types of words used (depending on the job description):

> Ability to implement
> Analytical ability
> Budget
> Business plan
> C++
> Clerical
> Data analysis
> Edit
> Financial reporting
> Forecast
> HTML programming
> Marketing
> Microsoft Word
> Policies and procedures
> Policy development
> PowerPoint
> Problem solving
> Product strategy
> Results oriented
> Schedule
> Software design
> Strategic planning
> Supervision
> Team player

Some phrases might include:
Under budget
Surpassed goals
Successfully developed

Check through job postings and ads carefully for keywords to use on your resume. You'll notice that keywords can easily be incorporated in your accomplishment statements.

Develop Accomplishment Statements

It's important to have accomplishment statements prepared for use in your resume and cover letter. An accomplishment statement is a detailed statement that lets the employer know what you've achieved in the past. These statements typically showcase your strong skills or values. Ideally, use work-related statements. If you do not have work-related statements, they can include volunteer work, applicable hobbies, and family experiences. If applicable to the job, you can use the accomplishment statements you already have on your Career Profile. Before you write your resume, spend some time writing accomplishment statements that are relevant to the job.

The following are action-oriented words to help you write accomplishment statements. They are used at the beginning of the statement:

Arranged	Evaluated	Presented
Calculated	Helped	Prioritized
Collected	Implemented	Produced
Computed	Installed	Programmed
Constructed	Led	Researched

Coordinated	Managed	Scheduled
Created	Motivated	Sold
Decided	Operated	Surveyed
Designed	Organized	Trained
Developed	Planned	Wrote

Here's are examples of accomplishment statements:

Skill: CREATE, DESIGN
Accomplishment Statement: Created marketing plans and designed brochures for the company's new product line.

Skill: IMPLEMENT
Accomplishment Statement: Implemented four new advertising programs on a yearly basis.

When you're ready to write your resume, you may want to combine your accomplishment statements as shown below:

Skills: CREATE, DESIGN, IMPLEMENT
Accomplishment Statement: *Created* marketing plans and *designed* brochures for the company's product line, and *implemented* four new advertising programs on a yearly basis.

Your accomplishment statements will help you write your resume!

From your Career Profile write down two of your strongest skills:
1. _____
2. _____

On the lines below, write your accomplishment statement for each skill. Be sure to start with an action-oriented word:

1. _____
_____
_____
_____

2. _____
_____
_____
_____

Now try combining two skills:

_____
_____
_____
_____

Now that you have some accomplishment statements, use them when writing your resume. Be sure that the accomplishment statements reflect what the employer is looking for.

More Tips for Writing Resumes

- Be honest! (People have ruined their careers by embellishing a resume.)
- Stay away from using words ending in –ing (use "scheduled" instead of "scheduling").
- Use results-oriented statements such as *"because of my problem solving skills.... the company was able to..."*
- Research the job you are applying for and use industry language on your resume.
- Do not include personal information on a resume such as age, ethnicity, or marital status.
- Do not list dates of employment older than 10 or 12 years ago unless you are re-entering the work force after many years. You may instead want to write, "Other relevant experience includes..."
- Be sure that the job experience you list is relevant.

How to Write a Resume

Here's an outline to help you write a basic combination resume. See examples of all three resumes on the following pages.

Personal Information:
Name, Address, Phone (including area code), Email

Objective:
State your employment goal. This is an optional category. Remember to change your objective each time you apply for a job. Be specific. For example, *To obtain a position as a training specialist focusing on web based training for administrative and managerial staff.*

Skills Summary (or use "Accomplishments" or "Summary of Qualifications"):

Your list should reflect what the employer wants. It should highlight your strengths. For example, if you are applying for a training specialist job: *Wrote and designed a web based training site for administrative staff; implemented on time and within budget.*

[Note: For a Functional or Chronological Resume, the "Skills Summary" category is not included.]

Education:

Begin with your highest degree and work backwards. List academic honors if relevant. List your education before the "Experience" category if you want to feature the degree or college and your education is your best qualification. Otherwise, include it after "Experience."

Experience:

Give the job title, place of employment, city, and state, and dates of employment (you may use years only).
Then, list accomplishment statements. Use your action words and results-oriented statements to describe your experience. Emphasize your strongest skills first. Try to directly relate your experience to the job you are applying for, using specific details. Include volunteer experience if relevant.

[Note: For a Functional Resume, only job functions would be listed here. In addition you would include another category called "Employment History")

Additional Information:

Community involvement or other training such as volunteer work, relevant hobbies, honors, awards, certificates, memberships, languages spoken. You may give this category a more relevant name if desired (i.e. Certifications, Memberships, Other Training).

Here's an example of a combination resume:

26 Cambridge Dr.
Lincoln, CA 62333
(424) 322-6922
sgomez@zol.com

Susanna Gomez

OBJECTIVE
To obtain a position as a training specialist focusing on implementation of web based training and classroom programs for administrative and supervisory staff

SKILL SUMMARY
- Planned, designed, and implemented training programs including the Administrative Excellence Series and New Employee Orientation
- Created, wrote, and designed web-based training sites including Managing Performance and Supervising Others
- Consulted with departments on performance management, leadership development, and organizational development

EXPERIENCE
Lincoln University   Lincoln, CA 1994–present
Training and Organizational Development
Training and Organizational Development Specialist
- Planned and implemented University-wide training programs for staff including vendor negotiation
- Designed curriculum and trained staff on skills including communication, problem solving, time management
- Created department web site, and web based learning modules for supervisory and new staff
- Consulted with departments on performance improvement and organizational development

Lincoln University   Lincoln, CA   1990–1994
Information Technology Systems and Services
Training and Communication Specialist
- Campus Readiness team member on the Human Resources software project implementation rolled out to the University in 1994.
- Developed and delivered communication to all staff and faculty regarding project rollout and training
- Delivered classroom training; wrote and developed web-based tutorials; consulted with departments on work process redesign

EDUCATION
College of Notre Dame Lincoln, CA
M.A. Public Administration, Human Resources Mgmt.
B.S. Human Services Administration, Magna Cum Laude

CERTIFICATIONS AND MEMBERSHIPS
Certifications: Business Process Improvement, Negotiating to Yes , Project Management
Member: American Association for Training and Development

References available upon request

Here's an example of a chronological resume:

Damien Graham

4222 Icon Drive   (651) 478-9999
Syracuse, FL   dgraham@compu.net

OBJECTIVE

To secure a position in marketing that will enable me to expand my areas of responsibilities and diversify my skills

EDUCATION

Stanford University, Stanford, CA
Bachelor of Science – Business Administration, Cum Laude

EXPERIENCE

Syracuse Medical Group, Syracuse, FL 2000 - present
Marketing Coordinator/Patient Relations

Coordinate and implement marketing efforts involving management, department staff, and advertising agents. Gather and analyze research results and develop future marketing plans. Coordinate and present patient focus groups on customer service. Write all internal news releases for marketing purposes.

Aquarius Medical Corp., Milpitis, CA 1998-2000
Product Marketing Associate

Assisted in the development of marketing plans for innovative medical devices. Developed new product marketing plans, sales strategies, and sales forecasts. Assembled and computed daily sales and inventory analysis reports.

Molecular Sciences Co., Sunnyvale, CA 1994-1998
Product Manager

Prepared business and marketing plans to include pricing, marketing strategy, and forecasting. Designed and implemented marketing plans for two markets. Monitored competitors and determined competitive trends.

ADDITIONAL INFORMATION

Foreign Language: French

References available upon request

Here's an example of a functional resume:

Betsy Chan

1488 Olmstead Rd., Curry, WI (855) 988-1422, bchan@zol.com

OBJECTIVE: A position that would utilize my experience as a commercial artist by contributing expertise in design and print production

EXPERIENCE:
- Developed visual concepts for ads, brochures, press kits, and logos
- Designed logos for corporate identity
- Consulted with clients to advance the creative process
- Oversaw print production including blue line and press approvals
- Supervised photography of products marketed to clients
- Stored graphics for over thirty major retail stores

EDUCATION:
Bachelor of Fine Arts degree
Academy of Arts, New York, NY

EMPLOYMENT HISTORY:
Design Plus, Curry, WI
   Designer   2002 - present
Litho Productions, New York, NY
   Artist   2001 - 2002
Freelance print designer   1996 - 2001
Camp Pendack, Curry, WI
   Art Instructor   1993 - 1996

ADDITIONAL
INFORMATION: First prize winner, Artist Magazine's 8th Annual Open Art Competition

References provided on request.

The Cover Letter

Cover letters provide you with the opportunity to present yourself in a more subjective way to a potential employer. A resume accompanied by a well-written cover letter makes a strong impact highlighting your top qualifications. It can make the difference between getting an interview or having the resume rejected. Cover letters should never be more than one page in length.

Before you write a cover letter:

- Read the job description carefully and make a list of the skills needed for the job.
- Make a list of your own skills that match the skills on the job description.
- Write an accomplishment statement for each skill that matches the job description. Relate your accomplishment statements to the skills the employer is looking for.

For example, the job requires web design experience. Your accomplishment statement: *Designed, coded, and launched 120-page commercial site for multimillion-dollar company with a national market base.*

Relate your accomplishment statement to the skill the employer is looking for: *My experience writing, designing, and launching commercial web sites helped my company achieve first time profitability and revenues from online sales of $200,000 for 2002.*

The Cover Letter

Here is an outline to help you write your cover letter:

Personal Information and Salutation:

Date, Name of hiring manager, Title, Address
Dear Mr./Ms._____, (Be sure to address your letter to the hiring manager. If you were not given the person's name, call the human resources department and ask for it.)

Introduction:

Capture the reader's attention. Create interest and introduce yourself. State what position you are applying for. Also let the interviewer know if someone suggested you apply for the position. Let them know why you want the job. (I am applying for this position because…)

The body:

Give an overview of your qualifications. Elaborate relevant accomplishments and qualifications. Choose the three most important skills you think they are looking for and write your accomplishment statements for each of these. Remember to relate your accomplishment statements to the skills they want.

This part should be 1 - 2 paragraphs. Include how you can make a contribution to the employer and why you want to join their company.

Closing:

Make a formal statement of commitment to the company or organization. Take initiative and state the next step you will take (when you will follow-up, the best way to reach you to set up an interview), and a thank you for taking the time to review your resume.

Remember to use your own "voice" in the cover letter. Your letter should not sound mechanical.

Sample Cover Letter:

May 16, 2003

Ms. Valerie Beckman
College of Bakersfeld
1444 Fielding Circle
Bakersfeld, CA 42333

Dear Ms. Beckman,

I am submitting my resume for the position of Training Specialist, Job # J011539 posted on May 1, 2003. I have over eleven years of experience designing and implementing courses and programs for staff, writing and designing marketing and communication materials, and consulting with departments and teams on performance and process improvement.

I am very interested in working with your team at a college that has been commended for its cutting edge training ideas and stellar implementation record.

In my present and previous positions, it has been the norm to work on multiple projects simultaneously. I always produce results and meet tight deadlines without supervision. My skills in communication, both written and oral have helped me to work effectively with all levels of staff, faculty and students. I am adept at analyzing a problem or situation, recognizing the pitfalls, and implementing a timely solution. Giving our clients the support they need is extremely important to me.

I would love to utilize my talents to ensure that your programs are implemented on a timely basis, and with positive results. I will contact you next Wednesday to set up time for us to talk further and explore the number of ways I can contribute to your department and the college's success. Thank you for taking the time to review my resume.

Sincerely,

Sandra Seeker

Now let's move to the job interview.

Interviewing: Your Elevator Pitch

Before your first interview, prepare a two-minute presentation using the categories below. Your pitch should short enough to recite to someone you meet during an elevator ride. Practice this pitch with a friend or someone on your networking list. You will also use this when they ask in an interview: "Tell me a little bit about yourself."

Summarize the following:

Your Education:

Your Experience:

Your Accomplishments:

Your Strengths:

Your two-minute presentation will help you to organize your thoughts and build your confidence before an interview. Studies show that when meeting someone for the first time, judgments are formed within four minutes and these judgments will affect subsequent impressions. Many recruiters have commented on candidates leaving a lasting impression in the first two to three minutes of an interview, so make this time count.

The Successful Interview

To be successful when interviewing for a job:

Be Conscientious – prepare as much as you can before the interview. Gather information about the organization, practice interview questions, and arrive early for your interview.

Be Confident – have a self-assured, positive, and upbeat attitude.

Interviewing can be a stressful process, but the most important things to remember are listed below. Successful interviewing is not as complicated as hundreds of books make it seem. You can go to the library and bookstores and look up scores of potential questions employers may ask you. It will be worth your time to only practice answering general questions. Knowing the answer to all the questions only helps if the employer asks that particular question!

Listening carefully to interview questions is just as important. In general, 80 percent of the interviews conducted have had a least one question answered by a candidate incorrectly, partially answered, or repeated for the candidate. This happens all the time. So, if you listen well in an interview, you will be better equipped to answer the question and stand out as an excellent communicator.

Becoming a better listener will not only help you in job interviews, but also on the job and in life. If you interview and don't receive an offer, it's disappointing, but you need to learn from the experience and move on to the next opportunity.

Listening and the Job Interview

Interviewing is a give-and-take process. Both you and the potential employer should listen carefully. The better you listen, the better the outcome.

- **LISTEN** to assess communication style (the person hiring you is soft-spoken or gregarious, confident or unsure of himself, formal or informal, knowledgeable or not).

- **LISTEN** to the kinds of questions you're being asked.

- **LISTEN** to the question carefully, so you can answer with specific examples.

- **LISTEN** for comments to assess the culture (what people seem to have in common in the workplace).

- **LISTEN** for negative comments about the work or people.

- **LISTEN** to how people interact with each other.

- **LISTEN** to find out if this is the job you really want.

INTERVIEWING CHECKLIST

Be prepared:

✓ With a calendar or notebook devoted to keeping track of interviews, name, location, and time. Always show up at least 10 minutes early for an interview to take a few deep breaths to de-stress and observe your surroundings.

✓ To dress appropriately for the interview. It is acceptable to ask the person who schedules your interview what the appropriate attire will be for the interview.

✓ To develop rapport as soon as you can with the interviewer.

✓ For an open-ended question at the beginning of the interview such as *"Tell us about yourself"* or *"Tell us about your career path."* You may choose to summarize the past five years or give your two-minute presentation (education, experience, accomplishments, strengths) as part of the answer to this question.

✓ To discuss the type of work you want and how your education, experiences, skills, and special talents relate to the job.

✓ For questions asking for examples of a time you used a particular skill or behavior needed for the job. Be prepared with concrete examples of how you previously used the skills advertised for the job.

✓ To describe the organization and know what they do.

✓ To explain why you want to work for them and what you can contribute.

✓ To sound enthusiastic and confident with a positive attitude.

✓ To be honest (never lie on a resume or in an interview).

✓ For surprise questions. Employers ask these questions to find out how you'll react in a stressful situation. It's all right to calmly say, *"Let me take a minute to think about that."*

✓ To always speak well of past employers. Future employers do not want to hear negative remarks because they will think they're next, if you leave the job.

✓ To talk about your future plans. Although the workplace is rapidly changing, employers want to know how long you plan on staying. It is acceptable to say that you will stay as long as the organization provides you with a challenging environment and opportunities to grow in your career.

✓ To let the employer know how much you want the job.

✓ To ask the interviewer well thought-out questions at the end of the interview.

✓ To thank the interviewer, shaking his/her hand and asking for a business card.

After the interview

Write a thank-you note that day clarifying or enhancing what you said in the interview. Again, let the interviewer know how much you want the job.

References

Most job interviewers will request references. Choose your references carefully! The following are guidelines for obtaining written and verbal references:

- Employers generally ask for two to three references. You will need to choose at least two that know you as an employee, and a personal reference that can comment on your character.
- It is acceptable to provide the person who is writing your reference with an outline of qualifications for the job. You may ask the person to focus on specific skills for the job you are applying.
- If you choose to have an employer contact a reference by phone or e-mail, be sure to inform your reference prior to your interview.
- Remember to thank your references whether you are offered the job or not. Your references may be able to provide valuable information by telling you what the employer asked about you. This may help you in future interviews.

Congratulations! You have finished all of the sections in this book. You know yourself quite well, have chosen a new career or identified careers to explore, honed your job search skills, and written your resume. You may even have turned the corner and obtained your dream job! The final chapter lists resources for further reading and research. Remember that this book can be used repeatedly – your values, skills, interests, and goals do change over time. Now that you have some good career skills, you have the tools to make a positive career transition! Good Luck!

Chapter 10

Resources

"Know then thyself, presume not the Web to scan until you know what you love to do, and have evolved a plan."
Richard Bolles from his website, www.jobhuntersbible.com

Websites

(Websites are constantly changing and what is on the Web today may be gone tomorrow. This list is current as of the publication date.)

Career Assessments

These sites will help you know yourself better. The assessments will give you an in-depth look at your skills, interests, and working styles, and help you explore career options.

www.jobhuntersbible.com
> Provided by Richard Bolles, author of *What Color is Your Parachute?*, includes free online tests, cool jobs, and self-employment information

www.self-directed-search.com
> The Self-Directed Search focuses on careers that match your interests (takes 15 minutes and costs less than $10)

http://www.discoveryourpersonality.com/Strong.html
> The Strong Interest Inventory test compares your interests to the interests of the people who enjoy their jobs

Also check local job services and state employment offices. Resources are often free of charge.

General Career Resource Information

These sites list general career resources including how to prepare for the job search, employment opportunities, and resume writing tips.

www.quintcareers.com
  Quintessential Careers
www.rileyguide.com
  The Riley Guide
www.wetfeet.com
  Includes career profiles and industry overviews

Careers and Skills

The site below includes job descriptions, and the skills needed for the job. Reading job descriptions on these sites helps you to understand what skills are needed for different careers.

http://online.onetcenter.org
  Department of Labor and Training Administration's *O*NET Online Dictionary of Occupational Titles* identifies over 1,000 job titles and is an updated version of the *Dictionary of Occupational Titles*

www.wetfeet.com
  Includes career profiles and industry overviews

Jobs

If you are looking for a job, these sites list job openings throughout the U.S. and how to apply. Most sites include general career information.

www.careerbuilder.com
http://hotjobs.yahoo.com
www.jobbankusa.com
www.jobdirect.com
www.monster.com

Exploring Market Conditions

These sites list job trends, labor market conditions, and future job outlooks.

www.bls.gov/oco

> online *Occupational Outlook Handbook*, which provides an overview of labor market conditions

www.next20years.com

www.wetfeet.com

> Includes career profiles and industry overviews

Exploring Wages

These sites list the average wages and benefits for a variety of careers.

www.bls.gov

> Includes labor statistics and wage information www.salary.com

Books

If you would like to read more books for job hunters and career changers, try these:

Change your Job, Change your Life, Ronald L. Krannich, PhD, Impact Publications, 2000

Wishcraft: How to get what you really want, Barbara Sher with Annie Gottlieb, Ballantine Books, 2003

Love it, Don't Leave It: 26 ways to get what you want at work, Beverly Kaye and Sharon Jordan-Evans, Berrett-Koehler Pub, 2003

What Color is Your Parachute?, Richard Bolles, Ten Speed Press, Berkeley, CA, 2002

Also check the public library and bookstores for a myriad of career books on writing resumes, cover letters, and interviews.

Occupational Outlook Handbook, Dictionary of Occupational Titles (DOT) and *Holland Occupational Codes* can all be found in your public library, on the internet, or at bookstores.

Appendix

Appendix: Career Profile

Your Life Goal(s):   Most Significant
                                            Accomplishments:

Top 4 Values: Personal Values:

Top 2 Personal Interests: Top 2 Interest Categories:

Work Environments: Your Passion:

Top 5 Skills: Top 2 Skill Categories:

Skills Needed for a Future Career

Top Working Style(s):   Motivators

Ideal Workplace Schedule: Long Term Goals

Short Term Goals   Careers To Explore

About the Author

Barbara is co-author of "A Fork in the Road: A Career Planning Guide for Young Adults." In her 13 years as a training and organizational development specialist at Stanford University, Barbara created numerous professional courses, web-based training courses, and career programs for university employees. One of her online courses, "How to Recruit Applicants," won a Cinema in Industry International award in 2001. She also has 20 years experience as a teacher, writer, artist, and human resources consultant.

Barbara has a Master's degree in Public Administration, B.A. in Human Resources Management, and training in art and design. Her varied careers from a ski instructor to occupational therapist to writer are examples of how you can mesh your skills and abilities to create jobs that you love.

Barbara has turned her attention to children's fiction and continues writing from her home in Palo Alto, CA.

Printed in the United States
23179LVS00005B/498